The Fundamental Investor

JEREMY DYER

THE
FUNDAMENTAL
INVESTOR

How Passive Real Estate Investing
Will Build Your Future

Text Jeremy Dyer

Design Francesca Romano

Copyright © Jeremy Dyer

Text is private and confidential

First print November 2024

CONTENTS

Foreword — 11

I The Blueprints: The Mindset Shift — 15

II Foundations: My Winding Path to Real Estate Syndication — 39

III The New Build: Starting Point Capital — 81

IV Framing Out — 125

V The Returns and Scaling — 187

About the Author — 217
Appendix — 219
Glossary — 223

"Fundamental"

Fundamental (adjective): forming a necessary base or core; of central importance.

Fundamental (non): a central or primary rule or principle on which something is based.

To the D6 Team,

You are my "why" – the reason behind my every endeavor and ambition. This book is dedicated to you, with a burning desire to pass along the life and investing lessons learned. May it guide and inspire you as we continue our journey.

FOREWORD

by Zach Haptonstall, CEO & Co-Founder, Rise48 Equity

If you want to better understand passive real estate investing, there is no better educator than Jeremy, and I am so glad he is writing this book. As a sponsor or operator of passive real estate syndication investment projects, I have worked with many fund managers—over 80, in fact. By far, Jeremy's knowledge and his affinity for real estate syndication have exceeded that of other capital partners.

Initially, I put Jeremy's strong performance in raising capital down to beginner's luck. But it soon became clear that his results were not only sustainable, but they were increasing exponentially. Had we been in the habit of awarding a Rookie of the Year award, it would have gone to Jeremy, but I have since learned how he has earned a bunch of those already.

Another fund manager introduced me to Jeremy. He was already raising money for real estate syndicators around the beginning of 2023, and I approached him to discuss an opportunity and a possible partnership.

Jeremy shocked me from the start. We had several calls before he agreed to partner with us during which he conducted full due diligence. He vetted us as though we were under strict surveillance. He wanted to know about our background and infrastructure, the performance of past assets, our property and construction management, our supply chain, and the debt structure. No stone was left unturned, and I admired his attention to detail.

In addition to his careful vetting, Jeremy invested his personal cash with us before he ever participated with us as a fund manager. He tested our performance by putting his own funds at risk. He wanted to put himself in the shoes of our limited partner investors before he partnered with his personal and professional network. He wanted to be comfortable and confident with our group before he recommended us to this network of investors.

Raising tens of millions of dollars is not easy. Many of the managers we work with are beginners at the outset. Some have never raised capital before, and we give them the opportunity to learn so that they can add value to our operations. Jeremy had no learning curve. He innately knew what to do and was confident he could raise over a million dollars from his personal and professional network.

"Sure, you can!" I said, sarcastically.

But Jeremy walked the walk. He had already invested passively in close to 30 deals himself, each with an average investment of over six figures before he started raising capital for us. He had multiple seven figures of his own cash passively invested with different sponsors, and he had witnessed several other sponsors in action.

Because of that, he understood the debt structure and the financials of the deals. The fact that he was investing himself lent him credibility when he approached other investors because he had skin in the game.

Most importantly, Jeremy has a personal touch. He is genuine and authentic, and he understands the sponsor-investor relationship. He knows how to manage investor expectations and how and what to communicate. He knows how to nurture over the long term and grow his investor network. He is the complete package.

As a sponsor in real estate syndication, I can tell you that now is the time to invest in this space. By investing passively in real estate syndication, you can achieve passive income, protect and grow your wealth, and enjoy tax benefits by doing nothing other than making a wise investment.

Over the last few years, interest rates have skyrocketed to the detriment of many sponsors who were caught off-guard. Now, there are deals to be had at a discount. It is a great time to be buying real estate, and the properties are performing extremely well, particularly in the multifamily space. With interest rates now much higher, it is not easy for people to buy homes, and many have no choice but to rent. That means that quality apartment buildings are in demand.

But what do I know? I am merely a sponsor. I will let Jeremy tell you all about the dynamics of real estate syndication because, as the expert, he will do a much better job than I.

Take it away, Jeremy!

Zach Haptonstall

Zach Haptonstall, CEO & Co-Founder, Rise48 Equity

I
THE BLUEPRINTS: THE MINDSET SHIFT

RISE SUN VALLEY

In partnership with Rise48 Equity, we are pleased to present Rise Sun Valley, a 323-unit multifamily investment opportunity in Dallas-Fort Worth, Texas.

The property offers immense upsides with the opportunity to renovate 100 percent of the classic interiors (323 units). The property was built in 1984 and is currently branded Briarwood Apartments, which will be rebranded to Rise Sun Valley. Rise Sun Valley is a B+ class asset located in a B+ class location of the Dallas-Fort Worth market.

This opportunity is unique in that Rise48 sourced this deal completely off-market with no competition from anyone else through a broker relationship. The property has been owned by a large private equity firm since 2019, and they must sell the deal to meet their five-year investment horizon.

The property is being poorly managed by the seller with below-market rents, which presents major operational upsides.

We are buying this deal at $108,000 per unit, which is the lowest price per unit of any deal we have bought in Dallas-Fort Worth. This represents a 25 percent-plus discount from what it would have sold for 12-18 months ago. Rents are well below market and represent significant upside potential.

This investment opportunity is a Reg D 506(b) offering, so it is open to both accredited and qualified non-accredited investors. We are accepting self-directed IRA funds for this investment opportunity. Please reach out if you are interested in exploring this option.

At 9:30 a.m. on February 1, 2024, my company, Starting Point Capital, issued a notice for a multifamily real estate investment opportunity. The opportunity was to assume and renovate a 323-unit multifamily property investment in the Dallas-Fort Worth market.

The investment notice invited accredited and non-accredited investors to enter into a limited partnership with a multi-family operating company with a proven track record and act as the general partner.

The business plan was a value-add, renovating all 323 units of an operationally distressed property and rebranding the property to Rise Sun Valley. The total offering size was over $22 million.

This was not my first rodeo raising funds for this general partner, but I was still a novice in their eyes. They were still not convinced that my past capital-raising efforts had not been flukes. This project was a big one, and $22 million was a huge amount of capital to raise. I had to admit that I was sweating, but I still clicked "send." The notice was now out to my network of investors. It was time to show the general partner that I could ride a bronco or two and not lose my hat because my head was too big or my seat not deep enough.

Just six hours after sending the notice, the deal was fully subscribed. My cell phone was blowing up, and my allocation of the $22 million of capital was already accounted for. That was a personal record.

I believe that there are many people out there looking for a new type of investing. You might be one of them and in a similar position to the one I found myself in a decade or so ago. I was fed up with the status quo—the Wall Street shenanigans, disappointingly low-interest CDs, lackluster life insurance policies, and other worn-out tenets of financial advisors. If you picked up this book, I would wager that you are probably a self-starter and not particularly risk averse. You have a good income, yet you are frustrated when grinding it out in your day job. You know there is a limit to what you can do working for someone else and are investing actively.

You might have an entrepreneurial itch you want to scratch and even have a business plan partially drafted, but you are hesitating because you know the risks. Starting a business is an option for more active investors, and the sky could be the limit if you have enough bandwidth in your life and are addicted to the grind. However, it is far from an easy side gig and takes a heck of a lot of work. You will probably have to work two jobs until you can make enough margin to leave your current employer and, again, it is high risk. If you have a family to support, a mortgage to pay, healthcare to worry about, and retirement funds to protect, it is a big leap to take. You are betting on yourself and the accumulation of transferable skills that you have developed over time.

So, what is the answer? In my case, the answer has been passive investing in real estate. Now, let me warn you that this is not an easy gig, either. Like any investment, you can lose all your money if you do not approach it with acquired knowledge, a best-in-class network, and due diligence.

This book will teach you about passive investing and in real estate syndications specifically. I will impart all that I have learned as I journeyed from a frustrated Wall Street investor to the founder and managing member of a company raising capital for real estate syndications. I was so blown away by the results that I had to jump in with both feet. I have now been around the block where real estate investing is concerned, and it all started with a mindset shift.

SHIFTING PERSPECTIVES

My mindset shift occurred at a time when I was living a good life, financially secure at the top of my game. Perhaps that is where you find yourself as you read this book. Like most Gen-Xers, I thought I was wedded to traditional investing styles, the humdrum of a strategy of a 401(k), stocks, ETFs, and life insurance, but I became increasingly disillusioned—and bored, frankly—by the lackluster performance of my portfolio. Then, when the 2008 financial crisis hit, I completely lost faith in the investing machine that is Wall Street and its droves of financial advisors and analysts. Seizing upon the real estate trend that followed the crisis, I dove into fixing and flipping, picking up cheap properties, renovating them, and selling them. I did not lose money fixing and flipping, but I did lose free time.

Frustrated anew, I searched for ways to make my money work for me that would not detract from my quality of life but add to it. I wanted to set myself up to be able to take a step off the hamster wheel for a second. How could I have more time and financial freedom to choose to do the things that I wanted to do?

I realized that I needed to create cash flow today rather than stashing my cash in a diversified portfolio and hoping that my returns would beat inflation. That is when I hit upon passive real estate investing. OK. Full disclosure. I was looking for some excitement and speculation—something to put my cash into that was not stocks, ETFs, and life insurance. I wanted a faster route to a place where I had more time to spend doing what meant most to me, which is spending time with my family.

My first investment in REAL ESTATE SYNDICATION was a multifamily property. In 2015, my wife Marlene and I put six figures of our own money into the deal. I knew enough about how single-family, value-add real estate worked but, if you had asked me back then what the word "syndication" meant, I would not have had a clue other than how I knew the Green Bay Packers are a syndicated football team.

> **REAL ESTATE SYNDICATION:**
> A syndication is a group of investors who come together to deploy capital into a project or property. In return for their capital injection, the investor group receives a portion of the cash flow the property produces and the equity upside at the end.

In retrospect, that first investment went surprisingly well, considering I largely used the shotgun approach, holding my breath and plugging my nose. I knew shockingly little about the world of general partners, capital stacks, and cash-on-cash returns—and how to de-risk such a deal—but you will if you read this book.

This book will show you what I discovered. I will explain the appeal of real estate syndication: Its wonders, its risks, why it is the salve I was looking for, and why it could be the right move for you.

Before we go there, however, I need to tell you more about me and the catalysts for my mindset shift. If you can understand and relate to my experiences, then what I say about real estate syndication will make more sense.

INFLUENCES

From an early age, I could sell just about anything. I started with candy bars for the Boy Scouts. Candy was an easy sell, but the problem was that they never gave me enough inventory, so I walked to the corner store to load up on Snicker bars and Reese's Pieces to continue my winning sales streak, adding on a slight margin for my efforts.

Later, in fourth grade, I sold Christmas wreaths and other household knickknacks around my neighborhood. My parents were both successful salespeople, and I came by the trade naturally.

Now, do not get the impression that this book is about selling. It is not. The purpose of this book is to educate others regarding the gift of real estate syndication. To do that in a convincing way, though, I have to tell my story and, to do that, I have to reveal what makes me tick, which is sales.

I did not come from a wealthy family, and I had no rich uncle, but my parents were extremely driven. I am sure that is part of the reason they separated when I was eight years old—they were just too similar. "They had grit" is how my wife, Marlene, describes them.

After my parents were married, two things happened. First, my parents both launched into their careers. My mother was hired as a sales rep for a well-known dairy brand called Land O'Lakes, and my father was a salesman in the high-tech software and hardware industry. Second, they had me. They were only 20 years old when I was born. Consequently, my mother did not go to college until later, and my father never went at all.

At the time, my mother did not see a problem with not going to college. "I needed to get out on my own," she told me. "I didn't want to go to school back then. I was in a place where I needed to earn a paycheck."

Later, when she hit a glass ceiling, she realized that a degree would help her to break through, so she went back to school. My mother had no lack of business sense, which was evident as Land O'Lakes soon became a local household name under her stewardship.

My relationship with my mother was antithetical to my relationship with my father. I was close to both of my parents, but I spent the bulk of my time with my mother so, naturally, most of the parental disciplining fell upon her shoulders.

"Have you done your homework, Jeremy? Is all your stuff ready for school, Jeremy?" My mother tried to keep me on the straight and narrow as far as school and life in general was concerned.

My father, on the other hand, focused on more immediate and exciting pursuits. He was a great life coach, and he recognized my efforts in school and in sports. He praised me and cheered me on, and I ate that up, but it was my mother who kept me accountable.

As I grew, I watched my parents' careers take off. My father was a larger-than-life character, and I was his biggest fan. I remember rooting for my dad to hit his quotas each year so that he could attend the annual quota club trip with his company. I made it a habit to check the whiteboard in his office where he monitored his sales. I marveled at the way he reverse-engineered his sales goals to figure out where the business would come from. Information technology was taking off at the time, and selling hardware meant that he was in the right place at the right time.

I was not the easiest of children, and I tended to find trouble although I did not really look for it. Children had much more freedom in the 1980s before helicopter parenting was a thing. I was a latchkey kid. My parents worked long hours, and I was left to my own devices much of the time. I learned to be independent. At the age of nine, I got myself up and ready for school and walked there unaccompanied. I walked home to an empty house after school, and my summers were endless days with limited parental oversight, which was similar to what many to most children experienced in the 1980s.

During those times of solitude, I learned to rely upon myself, which gave me confidence. I also learned to be a good problem-solver, which was useful because I created lots of problems. Strangely, I did not feel neglected—far from it. Despite many self-inflicted mistakes, my mother had my back.

As an illustrative example, when I was in fourth grade, one of my teachers had a system to keep us in line. She assigned naughty marks to the children who committed offenses. If you strayed from the straight and narrow, she ceremoniously drew a checkmark next to your name on the chalkboard for everyone to see, and the punishment was detention.

"Jeremy," she would say, "yet another checkmark for you."

I really did not care and, very late in the school year, I had accumulated so many naughty marks next to my name that there were not enough days left in the school year for me to serve my time. I just kept committing offense after offense after offense. In fact, I provoked the teacher. She saw it as a punishment; I saw it as a challenge.

I was in detention so often that my mother grew suspicious. If the system was designed to correct behavior, then why was I always in detention? Either this teacher was ineffective, she was picking on me for trivialities, or both. Either way, everybody's time was being wasted.

"Unless Jeremy's smoking cigarettes or hanging out in the girl's bathroom, I don't understand why he has to keep staying after school," my mother said.

I should add here that I had undiagnosed ADHD. I rarely stayed focused on a task at hand because there was always something more interesting on the horizon. ADHD has been both a gift and a curse—probably more a curse in my formative years when no one understood what it was.

Another reason I was so high achieving on the naughty board was that I was used to being free to make plans. Not only that, but I could move forward with them without any adult interference. In the classroom and at home, my plans and strategies were often not the best ideas, but I would plow ahead anyway and ask for forgiveness later. Right or wrong, that was how I operated. It was calculated, but I largely felt my way through situations, experiences, and decisions. I never hesitated.

I believe that I never lose. I only win or I learn. My fourth-grade teacher reinforced that belief with her system of checkmarks on the chalkboard. Each transgression that I committed was done because I knew it would bring me recognition, and the detentions were insignificant.

Why am I telling you all this? It is because I want you to know me and build confidence around my perspectives on investing. I have made investing decisions the same way I have made decisions all my life. By learning what works and what does not. I have pioneered real estate syndication investing for you. Navigated sensibly, I know that it is a safe path to follow and one paved with an opportunity to change your current wealth-building strategy.

FINDING BOUNDARIES

According to my mother, I was, and still am, motivated by both money and winning.

"Jeremy's interesting," a teacher once told my mother. "If he sees something he wants, he won't stop until he gets it. It's like he's always reaching for the carrot. I've never seen anyone so quietly determined."

My mother also said that I was a risk-taker, and I never considered the consequences of my actions or, if I did, I would go for it anyway. I cannot help myself.

I was rarely put off by obstacles because I did not recognize boundaries. How could I recognize boundaries? I had the autonomy of a 27-year-old—just without a car. If there are no boundaries, then there is no weighing of the pros and cons of crossing them. So, I invariably went too far. That led to plenty of disasters such as small grass fires I lit that turned into much larger fires.

"Jeremy, what were you thinking?" my mother would scold. "You've got to make better decisions."

At one point, I cut a hole in the baseboard in the living room to feign a mouse infestation.

"Mom! Look! I think we've got mice."

"Oh, it's probably an old hole," she said, optimistically. "I bet the mouse has gone by now."

The next day, I cut a new hole and pointed it out to my mother when she came home. I cut holes in the living room and then in the kitchen where I figured she might show more concern. I did it again the next day. By the third day, she finally seemed to care.

"Okay. We'll set some traps."

This all occurred just after my parents' divorce when my sister and I were in our younger years. My sister was six years younger than me. and I was expected to take care of her to some extent.

We witnessed some unpleasant scenes when my parents' marriage was unraveling, and I sometimes took my sister into a closet to shield her from some of the worst of it. It was traumatic for both of us. I could not get recognition for protecting my sister, but I could get it for finding mice.

My mother remarried. My stepfather, Paul, was an engineer and an indisputably positive role model. My mother was his first wife, and he had no children. Consequently, he was very invested in my sister and me.

My sister and I saw my real father every other weekend and one night a week, but that left many days in between. Having Paul show interest in the things I liked made a huge difference in my behavior at school and in life. He shared my passions, and I attribute much of my success to his guidance and support.

My mother and stepfather had another baby when I was 15. It was strange being 17 and graduating high school with a two-year-old sister!

When I was in the fourth and fifth grade, I started selling Christmas wreaths around the local neighborhood. I created flyers showing the various types of wreaths and had no problem going door to door selling them. I also shoveled driveways for people, raked leaves, and did some landscaping in the springtime. I found a couple of key accounts that paid me quite handsomely.

One elderly woman had a large property and loved flowers. She was also very lonely. She was so grateful for my gardening work and the few minutes that I spent chatting with her that she paid me $50 an hour in cash sometimes, and this was 30-some years ago in the late 1980s and early 1990s.

In middle school, although contraband, I progressed to selling Bazooka Joe bubble gum. I bought five-piece packs for 25 cents and sold either the whole pack for a dollar or an individual piece for 25 cents. I made out either way.

Sales suited me because I could both reach for carrots and earn money when I got them. Also, in sales, there is not just one carrot; there is a whole bunch waiting for you.

Selling the Boy Scout candy, the wreaths, and the landscaping services had felt like shots of adrenaline. I became addicted to seeing the money pile up and the recognition I received.

When I was in high school, my first job was working in a local retail store. I was 15 and wanted a car. My parents were quick to point out the practicalities and informed me that I would need to earn around $300 a month to own a car and save about $1,000 for a deposit. They offered to co-sign a loan with me and pay the insurance on the condition that I maintained good grades.

A year later, I transferred to work in a bank. Initially, I was a teller, but the bank quickly realized how they did not want me behind the counter anymore. They needed me out on the front lines soliciting customers.

I was rewarded for selling bank products like checking and savings accounts and CDs. I might get $10 for each closed sale. Because I was opening more accounts than anyone else, I was rapidly dispatched to grocery stores and other retail locations to sell accounts. I was glad to have the opportunity to show what I could do.

A colleague and I set up a stand in the grocery aisle replete with brochures, balloons, and other paraphernalia to show that we were legitimate representatives of the local bank. I would query shoppers as they came by looking for their favorite cereal. "Do you like that type of Cheerios, or do you like the honey nut better?"

Complimenting people was a particularly effective conversation starter. "I like your red shoes. Where did you get those?" I knew that, if I could get someone to a point where they engaged in small talk, and I had their attention, it would be easy to transition to a more productive conversation.

"So, where do you bank today? Have you ever considered opening up an account? Today, we're giving away some cool promos. You can get a brand-new cooler if you open up an account, or we'll make your first $10 deposit into your bank account for free."

Without gaining that initial trust, no one is going to listen to your sales pitch.

As a result of my relentless persistence, I quickly became the number one guy in the branch office, the number one guy in the Twin Cities where we lived, the number one guy in the state, and then the number one guy in the Midwest. Oh, and I got the car. It was an amazing car, too—an electric blue Grand AM GT with subwoofers, amplifier, and personalized license plate. It had alloy wheels, a cool spoiler, and a moonroof.

> Without gaining that initial trust, no one is going to listen to your sales pitch.

In high school, I became somewhat of an enigma because I was not *trying* to be something. On the one hand, I had a cool car and was earning a ton of money compared to my peers. That was how I was perceived outwardly at least. But, on the inside, I was more genuine. I preferred hanging out with the unpopular kids because they usually had more substance. I was on the receiving end of some bullying because I attracted attention, but I was good at blocking it out. My wife says I use the turtle shell mentality. When I face adversity, I go into my shell and refuse to let it affect me.

In high school, I was president of the DECA chapter. DECA stands for Distributive Education Clubs of America. It is a volunteer-led association for sales and marketing students.

Students learn how to conduct sales demonstrations, gain interviewing skills, and discover how to market products and services and how to create a business plan. In addition to presiding over the DECA chapter and competing nationally in sales competitions, my role was to reach out to small, medium, and large businesses and land $5,000 checks to sponsor our DECA chapter.

It was around this time that I met my future wife, Marlene. I was the teaching assistant in a class that she attended. She later joined DECA and was paired with me as her "big brother." I hooked her up with a job at a different local bank branch, and Marlene was also sent out into the field to sell. I assured her that she would love the job. I was wrong; what had been sales nirvana for me was sales torture for Marlene.

"I hated approaching someone picking out a pound of apples and asking them if they wanted a checking account," she said. "It seemed so invasive."

Marlene was much happier as a teller. Seeing her visceral reaction to a situation I reveled in was illuminating. I realized that my approach was different.

I would go on to work at the bank all the way through college.

It was not all smooth sailing, though, in those early days. As much as sales was a strong string to my bow (I had my sights set on business school because of it), academically, I was a hot mess. I scored a 17 the first time I took the ACTs and, when I took the test again, I got the same score! Initially, I hoped I had just had a bad day but, nope, I really was that bad. My test-taking abilities were abysmal. I suffered terribly from test anxiety. If I were taking a test, I could start to read a question and, by the time I got to the end of the sentence, I could not remember how the sentence had begun. Then, I would start to panic as the clock would wind down.

I entered a program at the University of Minnesota. It was called the General College, or GC program, which was the lowest-level entry point. It was not even the mainstream liberal arts program. It was a separate program created for students with poor ACT scores.

Marlene and I were dating by this time, and she attended the same school and carpooled with me. Marlene had scored 17 in her ACT test also and, when she took it again, she got 16. I loved her for that! She went on to get a bachelor of arts degree in history and a masters degree in education, and she became a high school teacher.

"Test scores are overrated," she would tell you.

As a freshman, I was probably the most laser-focused student that school had ever seen because I was so determined to graduate. I obliterated distractions. I did not get involved in fraternities, I did not get involved in extracurricular activities, and I made the decision to live at home and commute.

For me, college was just another box to check off, and I wanted the boxes checked as quickly as possible. I had no interest in experiencing college life. I wanted to move on. I had things to do. I felt that three-quarters of my education was completely worthless, so I might as well get it over with and find out what life was really all about. I feigned interest in geology, calculus, and statistics, but it was purely to get the grade and take the next class on the list. I just wanted to get my GPA high enough for acceptance at the Carlson School of Management, a prestigious undergraduate and graduate college within the University of Minnesota that was ranked sixth or seventh among business schools in the country.

My first year at the University of Minnesota, I studied so hard. I made sure that, when the dreaded exams came around, I did not clam up, freeze, or panic. One panacea was drinking Mountain Dew. The caffeine, which is a component of many ADHD medications, saved me on test days.

My work paid off in my freshman year, and I was accepted into the Carlson School during my sophomore year. I was thrilled. I had wanted to major in marketing and sales since I was eight years old. Then, as a senior, I attended an on-campus job interview with ADP, a leading provider of human resources management software and services, and they hired me on the spot. That was a relief because I had made a bad decision financially during my time at the University of Minnesota.

BUBBLES AND MARGINS

Trying a new investing venture is not something I shy away from. I am drawn to new ideas. When I was a junior in college, thinking I could make it with the next best thing, I tried my hand at day trading. I opened my first online trading account with E*TRADE and went merrily into the land of candlesticks and fundamentals. I had some winners and some losers, but the real challenge came when I invested in speculative tech stocks.

At first, it was all too easy. *This is great!* I thought. *I can invest a thousand bucks in a tech stock and sell it for $1,500 in 30 days. That's a 50 percent return!* Rinse and repeat. I spent a lot of time researching companies and, frankly, gambling.

In my senior year, I picked a winner. I bought a stock for 25 cents a share, and that stock shot up to $60 per share. I had a 23,900% return. Beat that! Then I got greedy and did not sell. I figured the stock was going to the moon, and I was going to make a million bucks. I was ready to ride off into the sunset and never look back.

I held the stock and, before I knew it, the price tanked from $60 a share to 85 cents per share. That lesson hurt, so I doubled down trying to find the next winner. My strategy was to buy low, sell high, and not get greedy. I foolishly started using my college tuition to trade and, worse, I started to trade on margin. I was trading with borrowed money, which meant any losses that would inevitably follow would only be amplified.

At that point, the speculative tech bubble started to burst. Not only was my college tuition going up in smoke, but my losses were amplified because I was trading on margin and leveraging against my very own college tuition!

"Jeremy." Marlene looked at me with a concerned and pitying look as I sat at my makeshift trading desk. "This is not the way. There are other options, but you have to stop the bleeding on this one."

She was right and, in fact, my being consumed by day trading was having a negative impact on our relationship. This was one lesson I learned in spectacular fashion—that not all scratches need to be itched, and not all shiny objects need to be chased after.

PLATINUM HANDCUFFS

Studying for an MBA never made sense to me. I had always wanted to be in sales, not upper management where you avoided the front-line work. I have to be the guy working directly with the customer, building the relationship. I cannot be the guy in the corner office telling the troops how to do their job. I know they cannot do it as well as I can, anyway.

After graduating from college in the spring of 2001, I began my career at ADP working in sales. This was a period in my life when I managed to curb my desire to push for the next thing. I drank lots of coffee and put my head down and worked as hard as I could. I also married Marlene and was on the cusp of starting a family. I recognized how this was no time to make rash decisions or change course without a justifiable reason.

ADP paid me well. I saw people around me come and go while I stayed. It was easy to establish myself, and taking a risk with a new company seemed foolish. I had a great base salary, an excellent commission structure, and incentives. How could I ever leave? I could not. I realized I was shackled to the job—not with gold handcuffs but platinum—keeping me bound to my duties because of huge commission checks, annual bonuses, a great stock purchase plan, stock options, a generous 401(k) match, and excellent health insurance. I was the labradoodle sleeping at the foot of my employer's plush bed. I knew myself well enough to know that I could milk this during my children's formative years, but it would not be long before I would be looking for the next opportunity.

Most of us who were brought up in the 1980s cling to the traditions of middle-class America. Our path was to study hard, work hard, get married, and provide for our families financially and emotionally. I was part of that demographic and, where my finances were concerned, I adhered to the advice of my parents and financial advisor. I needed to make sure my family was set financially so that I had some wiggle room later in case I wanted to try riskier investments, entrepreneurialism, or whatever else would float my boat.

"Okay, Jeremy," my financial advisor told me. "Let's get you set up with a diversified portfolio. You know, stocks, bonds.

We'll max out your 401(k) and get you some indexed universal life insurance. If you're feeling really devilish, we can grab you some crypto, a few nice art items if you are so inclined, maybe a Rolex or Patek Philippe or two." Sound familiar?

For a hot second, I went with it. My ADHD was under control thanks to my newfound love for good coffee, and I was achieving my financial goals thanks to my success at ADP. However, that did not last long. I got bored with the mediocre returns from Wall Street, and I soon had an insatiable thirst for some real excitement and speculation.

By the time I was 22, I was named Rookie of the Year at ADP for the entire Midwest. I claimed the top spot in my division in my second year and became number one in the country for sales, chasing a $1.5 million quota. I was an anomaly, and every other top sales performer was in my rearview mirror. Year after year, I had tag-alongs for ride days, and the company modeled training and incentive programs on my sales strategies.

"Jeremy," a vice president told me, "we want you to do a masterclass series. We want to call it your 'Blueprint for Success.' We thought you could pass on some of your sales wisdom to the other teams. Build into our sales force. What do you say?"

What I really wanted to say to the sales newbies was to buck the system, ignore the in-house sales protocols, and use their intuition instead. Build relationships and learn how to interact with clients authentically—meaning in a way that connects with them. I produced and presented the masterclass, trying to be politically correct without encouraging antithetical behavior.

As I said, at ADP, I was on top of my game professionally. I quickly built and paid off our family's dream home, acquired the 40-foot-class Super-C motorhome, and became a father to two wonderful children. I later became a father of four when we adopted, but I will go into that later. I was incredibly busy yet becoming incredibly bored. Now that I was comfortable, financially and professionally, and I had the perfect family, I needed the next fix. But what was it?

It did not take long for me to find it. But there was a problem. It was now 2008 when the world began to reel in the catastrophe that became a global financial crisis. At that point, things began to unravel for me financially. Like many others, I watched my portfolio plummet, and I fired my financial advisor.

The shift in my thinking was reaching completion at that point. I had seen enough, I knew there had to be a better way to use my money, and I was going to find it.

11
FOUNDATIONS: MY WINDING PATH TO REAL ESTATE SYNDICATION

"Sometimes, it sounds fantastic, Jeremy. I really appreciate your taking the time to explain it. It's just that real estate is a huge leap, you know? And $50,000 is a lot to put in one bucket. Let me take some time to think about it."

That is how many people react to the idea of passive real estate investing before they experience a shift in thinking. And I get it. You *should* hesitate before taking action, just not for too long.

There is a syndrome I see many people fall into when it comes to decision making, particularly financial decisions. People become paralyzed because they over-analyze things—paralysis by analysis. It is understandable that, when investment or business decisions are on the table, you might be hesitant because the outcome will affect your whole world. However, when considering whether to invest in something, there is a balance between understanding the risk involved and then actually taking the risk.

Many of my friends never get out of the starting block. They have the education and the ideas; they might even have a plan of what they want to do. They just lack the ability to get started. The sad thing is that they do not fulfill their dreams because they fear the unknown or making a mistake, or they worry that things will not go the way they want them to go.

Of course, you have to be able to afford to lose the funds if things go wrong. Warren Buffet's golden rule of investing is "don't lose money." The second rule of investing is to not forget the first rule. But, if you have the money, at a certain point, you have learned what you need to learn, you know what you need to know, and you take the plunge if the opportunity meets your risk-reward profile.

I see so many people who still do not take the plunge even if the signs are all positive. Instead of getting started, they cannot get beyond paralysis by analysis. That has never been a problem for me. In telling you my childhood narrative, I have been transparent in that I am wired to make a mess and clean it up later. Most adults try hard not to make a mess in the first place. And I have probably been lucky. But, whatever the reality, at some point when it comes to changing your wealth-building trajectory, you have to take an informed risk.

I admit that, to some, my way is high risk. When I had the cash to lose, my wins were big. But I also had big losses—just not in passive real estate investing. Day trading was certainly not my forte.

For me, finding a new path was the result of a mindset shift that I could not control. I poked holes in the Wall Street tropes and the advice I received from my financial advisor. In a nutshell, I realized that, instead of focusing upon how much I needed to save to retire—two million, five million, ten million—I needed to focus upon increasing cash flow today. Because, if I had more CASH FLOW today, I could make it work for me now and grow my wealth more quickly than if I could find the right investments.

> **CASH FLOW:** The income generated from a real estate investment after deducting expenses such as mortgage payments, property management fees, and maintenance costs. Positive cash flow indicates that the property is generating more income than its expenses.

THE PENNY DROPS

When I focused on an end figure, achieving a certain amount of wealth to retire, the goal post kept moving. The more I earned, the more assets I had and the higher my standard of living became. Throw inflation into the mix, and then that nebulous figure I needed to have before I could retire kept growing. For example, when I was in junior high, I thought that, if I could build a nest egg of a million bucks, I could retire. By the time I got into college, that goal post had moved, and one million had become two million. When I started a family, the goal post moved again. Now, I was at two-and-a-half million. Today, that nest egg number is probably five-plus million.

Why does the nest egg number move? It is because of lifestyle creep and inflation. When I was a child, you could get a value meal at McDonald's for $2.99. Now, a value meal is close to $10. So, I now look through a different lens and, if you look at things through a different lens, you can find a path to wealth that makes much more sense, and the outlook is much more attainable.

For example, if you look at what you make currently, you can figure out how to free up cash now, make the right investments, factor in inflation, and use that cash today to create more cash flow that will build wealth on an ongoing basis in the future. You can put your money to work and hedge against the inflation monster.

Are you financially secure with $50k or $100k sitting in CDs and IRAs? Those funds are earning minimal interest, so why not invest the cash you do not need in the next five years into a risk-adjusted passive real estate investment, making a five-time greater return that is tax-advantaged? The reason could be that you are stuck in a mindset of traditional investing.

You might believe that investing in stocks and bonds, maxing out your 401(k), and front-loading index life insurance policies is the way to go. I did, and so do most financial advisors. But here is the question: If that is the road to wealth, then why are so many financial consultants still grinding out a day job at age 60? Why are they not retiring and enjoying a mai tai on the beach? Maybe the Wall Street way is not as effective as you have been told.

Everyone should ask these questions. When you challenge the norms, that is when a mindset shift occurs. A few years ago, I spent a lot of time in the winter months as an assistant hockey coach because my three boys were all hockey players. I coached kids from the ages of three all the way up to 16.

I was always considered to be the mental coach, the sports psychologist if you like, as opposed to the coach strategist with the Xs and Os and the puck angles. My role was to reset a player's mental space if they were having a tough game. I would get them to look at the big picture, figure out how to manage the challenges, and find the opportunities instead of dwelling upon the negatives. I would see a player feeling totally beaten in the early stages of the game but, when I presented a new strategy to them, they would go back out onto the ice with a different perspective and often turn their game around.

My point here is that, once you take the time to reset your mind and really think about why you are doing things—and the reset makes sense—then you challenge yourself to make changes. Sometimes, it is easier not to do this and to stick with the status quo. But you cannot expect results if you refuse to think critically or analytically, or you choose to procrastinate.

If you sense that you are missing something in your investing strategy, you are right. What you are missing is a new way of looking at your relationship with money. Passive real estate syndication is a new concept that turns conventional investing strategies upside down.

In the next section, I will explain what happened when I turned my sights to passive investing.

AWAKENING

I have always had a sense of urgency. When ADP first recruited me at college, I convinced them to give me all of their materials and training so that I could get all the pre-work done and out of the way, unpaid. That way, I could hit the ground running on day one. I wasted no time. It is how I am wired. A sense of urgency is essential to take your game to the next level. If you operate with a sense of urgency in the business world, it can be a game changer with massive results.

That said, while a sense of urgency has proven a superpower for me, I also consider it my greatest weakness. Quite frankly, I am jealous of people who can turn the tap on and off and not live their lives thinking that everything requires their immediate attention.

ADP's sales model was nothing out of the ordinary, but my sense of urgency meant that I had balked at the system and followed my own instincts instead. I called people and knocked on the doors of small businesses, day in and day out, to stimulate activity and, ultimately, deals.

Never talk about the weather or your family, the ADP model warned. Well, I did completely the opposite. I always talked about the weather, and I always talked about my family because I wanted to build a connection with a potential client. I would even talk politics if that was the direction the conversation went. Nothing was taboo. I needed to convince the person that I was authentic and trustworthy and that their interest and business investment in me was well-placed. Only then was it worth asking questions about their needs. The sales model totally missed that vital nuance.

Once a client opened up to me, I consulted with them. I helped them to uncover pain points in their business—many did not even know they had them—and then I suggested different ways to relieve those pain points. It was always a thrill for me to get people to drop their guard to the point where I was a trusted confidant and advisor, someone with whom they were willing to show their cards and have a genuine conversation with. Getting to that point with someone requires choosing a path and, for me, it was not following the norms and traditions. I felt the same way about my investing. I felt a sense of urgency and a desire to do things differently.

I thrived at ADP; meanwhile, my life with Marlene was also rapidly evolving. We had tied the knot when we were just

23, and we had our first child when we were 27. We traveled, established our careers, and settled into midlife.

By the mid to late 2000s, I had a wonderful family with two beautiful boys, and Marlene and I had built our dream home and had the 40-foot RV sitting in the driveway. We had also paid off the mortgage (a sizable, 30-year fixed mortgage with a low interest rate of 3.9 percent paid off in 36 months). That was a mistake. In retrospect, I should have taken my excess cash and invested it in cash-flowing real estate where I could have earned a significantly higher, tax-advantaged return. But it was peace of mind that won that day.

I was set financially, yet I was questioning the traditional models built around Wall Street investing that no longer made sense to me. I was bored with it all. My parents believed that you save, invest in CDs and money market savings accounts, and pay off your high-interest debt. We learned to invest in commodities, precious metals, or a passbook savings account, which I do not think even exists anymore. That was the investing mindset I had going through college and in my early days of starting a family.

But none of it makes sense. Let us be honest. Financial advisors are selling Wall Street products. The financial advising community is composed of thousands of advisors working for Northwestern Mutual, Charles Schwab, Fidelity, or Vanguard to name just a few, and they receive a commission for doing so. They get paid whether your stocks go up or down. The truth is that many financial advisors are in their early twenties and fresh out of college. They have a college degree, they took a financial test, and they passed a background check. Now, all of a sudden, you are supposed to trust their financial advice? Stocks would go up on bad news, and stocks would go down on good news. Your financial advisor has a conflict of interest, fiduciary or not. Trust me, I know.

I decided to trust myself rather than my financial advisor. I read books and listened to podcasts from trustworthy sources. (I still listen to a dozen hours' worth of podcast content every week, and I learn from guests on my own podcast, *The Freedom Point Podcast*.)

Do not get me wrong, I had a great relationship with my financial advisor for a long time.

"Jeremy, I think you need to look at this ETF," he would tell me when we connected once a quarter over coffee or lunch. "Jeremy, I think you need to front-load this index fund."

But, then, the global financial crisis loomed, and everyone's world rocked.

"My portfolio just took a one-third haircut," I told my advisor in the thick of the crisis in 2008. "What do you think we should do?"

"Jeremy," he said. "I'm literally hiding under my desk right now. Let me get back to you."

I could not believe my ears. *Get back to me? My finances are collapsing, and you'll get back to me? These people have absolutely no idea what they're doing*, I thought.

Stocks were plummeting, and so was my home's value. This had not been part of my financial plan. Thankfully, I was in a good space with my day job at ADP, and I was mortgage-free, but I felt disenfranchised. I was doing what everyone else was told to do by the Wall Street marketing machine, and it all amounted to what felt like a con.

The global financial crisis woke me up. I saw that the system did not work, at least for me and probably many others in a similar situation. I felt like I was grinding it out, day in and day out, but not making any progress. Sure, I was debt-free, but how could I best set myself up to be financially free and able to take a step off the corporate hamster wheel for a second?

When people think about financial independence, they think about retirement. The focus is so much on the nest egg. People look at their 401(k) balance and their Fidelity stock portfolio, add up the numbers, and ask their financial advisor what their nest egg number needs to be. The problem is that you will always be chasing a new number because of inflation realities.

BEATING INFLATION

Inflation is one of our greatest taxes because it provides no value to anyone with the exception of the borrower (more on this later). The value of a dollar is cut in half approximately every 30 years. Lifestyle inflation also causes us to spend more on luxury items like airplane tickets and meals out because we expect our quality of life to improve despite the effect of inflation. Thus, we need to change the narrative to wealth preservation.

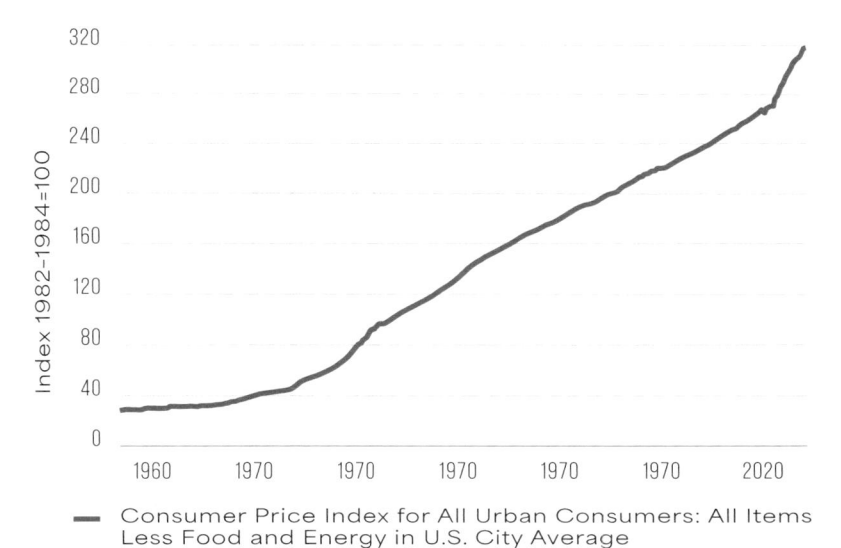

— Consumer Price Index for All Urban Consumers: All Items Less Food and Energy in U.S. City Average

Source: U.S. Bureau of Labor Statistics

It is not always about how much you make but how much you keep and how much of that retained money you can put into a wealth-building strategy that is a hedge against inflation. Recently, we have had such bad inflation that higher net worth individuals who could have walked away from their active income at a not-too-distant point now need to stay in the workforce another five years. Inflation has eaten away at their purchasing power and, unless they are willing to settle for a lower standard of living, they are being forced to remain dependent upon active income.

During the COVID epidemic, the federal funds rate or overnight rate set by the Federal Open Market Committee (FOMC) was lowered to 0.5 percent. The federal funds rate is now called the Secured Overnight Funding Rate (SOFR). It is the interest rate that United States banks pay one another to borrow or loan money overnight. It also affects interest rates on everyday consumer products such as credit cards or mortgages.

In 2021, post-COVID, the Federal Reserve Bank started increasing that rate drastically. There were around 11 rate hikes and, at the time of writing, the Fed funds rate was around 5.5 percent. The reason the SOFR is so important is that the government makes money in two ways. The first is inflation, and the second is taxes.

The United States has an enormous amount of debt, and debt is not always a bad thing. The fact that the world owns our debt means that we can leverage our debt and use it to influence global policies. United States' debt can only be paid back in U.S. dollars. However, if the United States maintains $30 trillion worth of debt, inflation decreases the impact of that debt.

I mentioned that it was a mistake for me to pay off the mortgage on my house. Why? Because the mortgage on my house at one point had an interest rate of 3.9 percent. When inflation is running at three to four percent, that loan is essentially free money. So, why would I take the value of a dollar today and buy down the debt on my own single-family home with a 3.9 percent interest rate when I could use that cash and invest it somewhere else and create tax-advantaged recurring cash flow?

There is velocity in money. When money sits stagnantly, it tends to lose value over time. Whereas, when you have money invested into hard assets or things that pay monthly recurring income through cash flow, you can stay ahead of the inflation curve. The opportunity cost of investing in a hard asset is a better decision than blindly rolling the dice on Wall Street.

Some people assume that they will change their lifestyle when they move into retirement. They no longer have kids at home, so they will downsize. But who really wants to do that? If anything, you will probably want to have a better lifestyle—more room in the home for visiting family and enough money to take trips and do things that you could not do when you were working an active, full-time, corporate job or running a business that owned you versus you owning it.

So, the mental change for me was to focus on how much passive income I needed to create enough cash flow on a monthly or annual basis to retire off that number. I can use that monthly recurring cash flow to completely replace my dependence upon my active income. That cash flow will pay my living expenses, keep up with inflation, and take care of lifestyle creep.

Just after the housing crisis, homes were selling for low prices. Television channels, like HGTV, cashed in on popular shows featuring property renovations and fixing and flipping as low home prices attracted people to the real estate market.

Marlene and I loved these shows—so much so that we hopped on the flipping bandwagon in 2012.

FLIPPING IS AN OPTION BUT NOT FOR EVERYONE

In 2012, when I was hankering after a new investment scenario, flipping, as seen on HGTV, seemed like a super sexy idea.

I was still grinding out a high-performing sales job but, at the same time, Marlene and I started a real estate investing company that focused on buying and renovating distressed single-family homes. Initially, we considered it a way to replace our dependence upon Marlene's income as a public school teacher. A fix-and-flip business allowed Marlene to stay at home with our two young boys, so this was a good fit for us. My father was a general contractor, and Marlene just happened to have a knack for interior design. We had a ready-made house-flipping team and were ahead of the game.

We started purchasing single-family distressed homes, many of which were in foreclosure or belonged to severely distressed sellers. We had a competitive advantage right off the bat because we submitted offers with no contingencies and no inspections, and we did not require bank financing. We were literally throwing cash at these properties and beating out the competition.

The properties were in unimaginably bad condition. In some cases, the yard had not been cut in three months. The gutters literally had maple trees growing out of them. Some houses went on the market looking like there was a meth lab inside and, in some cases, there were.

Not everyone is capable of profiting from flipping. Many get into the business and fail because they lack knowledge. The economy plays a role, too. If valuations and single-family homes in that market are declining while you are trying to force value appreciation through renovation efforts, those two can work against one another.

For example, there is a difference between forced appreciation and organic or natural appreciation. When organic appreciation occurs, the price of a single-family home might go up three and a half percent a year on average. But, guess what? That is the average. Some years, they might go up by eight percent and, some years, they might go down by six percent.

When you renovate a property, you increase its value. That is forced appreciation. If you buy right, then these forces work with one another. For example, in certain markets in this country, like Phoenix and the Sunbelt regions, prices have skyrocketed, post-COVID, because people realize that they can have their day jobs and live anywhere. So, they are flocking to these areas. Fix and flip in one of these areas and, if you're lucky with market timing, then you might hit the jackpot by benefiting from organic and forced appreciation at the same time. For comparison purposes, the "boring" Midwest markets have also fared well over the same period, but the fluctuations in valuations have not been so extreme.

We were lucky, and flipping became a rinse and repeat exercise that we capitalized upon. Still, we were rookies and, like most flipping rookies, we underestimated the time that it took to actually renovate these units. We also found that there were significant silent costs. Far from providing passive cash flow, I was actively engaged and working more hours than ever. I also had less time with my family.

The straw that finally broke the camel's back was the last property we flipped. We were set to make $70,000 in profit, but the profit was cut in half because, when it came time to sell, the inspector told us that the well and septic system had failed. We fixed it, but it cost $35,000—half of our profit.

We finally chose to exit the business in 2015. The blood, sweat, and tears were not what we were looking for. But there was a valuable lesson learned from our active investing in real estate fixing and flipping, which was why it had worked. We were eager to learn and had the right team.

This worked because I was the underwriter and check writer, my father was the contractor and property manager, and my wife was the interior designer. We had all the knowledge and expertise we needed to find the right property, create a new design, and execute the work. Because of our team, we did not lose money flipping and, as you will learn, that is *the secret* to passive investing in real estate syndications—the operating team.

In their book, *Passive Investing Made Simple: How to Create Wealth and Passive Income Through Apartment Syndications*, the authors Anthony Vicino and Dan Krueger use an effective analogy for a commercial real estate syndication, which is to think of it as an airplane ride. There are pilots, passengers, flight attendants, air traffic controllers, mechanics, and more who all work together to get the plane safely to its destination.

In this analogy, the pilots are the sponsors, or operators, of the syndication, and the passengers are the passive investors. They are all going to the same place, but they have very different roles in the process.

If unexpected weather patterns emerge, an engine has issues, or there is turbulence, the pilots are responsible for the flight. The passengers have no active responsibilities in making the decisions or flying the plane.

Imagine the pilot of a plane as the team operating a real estate project. Whether or not the project is successful, or whether or not you reach your destination safely, depends upon the expertise of the pilot and their ability to make good decisions.

After fixing and flipping, I started looking for the next opportunity and perhaps a bit of an adrenaline rush, too. Money market accounts were offering around half a percent with inflation at three percent. I knew I was losing money keeping my funds where they were, and I wanted to put my money into real estate where I could hedge against inflation, generate consistent cash flow, and build generational wealth. But, how?

> **PASSIVE REAL ESTATE INVESTING:** An investment approach where individuals invest their money in real estate projects but do not actively participate in the management or operations of the property. Instead, they rely upon professional syndicators or sponsors to handle the day-to-day activities.

WHY RICH PEOPLE INVEST IN REAL ESTATE

Before I explain how I found PASSIVE REAL ESTATE INVESTING, let me first explain what passive real estate investing is and why so many rich people are attracted to real estate syndication in particular.

Passive investing, in the broad sense, is a buy-and-hold strategy. The goal of passive investing is to build wealth gradually without making frequent trades or having to be actively involved. Passive real estate investing is a way to make money by investing in property without dealing with the dreaded four Ts—tenants, trash, toilets, and termites—which are problems the traditional active real estate investor faces.

Wealthy investors are attracted to passive real estate investing because they can participate without sacrificing time and because the financials make sense. Multifamily real estate investments have outperformed other asset classes, such as stocks and bonds, for years. Even during the Great Recession of 2008, multifamily real estate performed well above other asset classes. In 2008, the multifamily sector returned 5.2 percent, according to Freddie Mac, while the S&P 500 index *declined* by 37 percent, according to McKinsey.

The following chart was created by Roers Companies, a multifamily real estate investment, development, construction, and property management real estate company. It compares the volatility of stocks (S&P 500), bonds (Bloomberg Aggregate), public real estate trusts (NAREIT), private commercial real estate (NCREIF), and multifamily real estate (CoStar Multifamily) since the year 2000.

The chart below shows that stocks and publicly traded REITs experienced the most volatility. Bonds held steady throughout—nobody got rich, but they did not lose everything, either. However, multifamily real estate investments, which are not correlated to the stock market, showed the least volatility.

JEREMY DYER

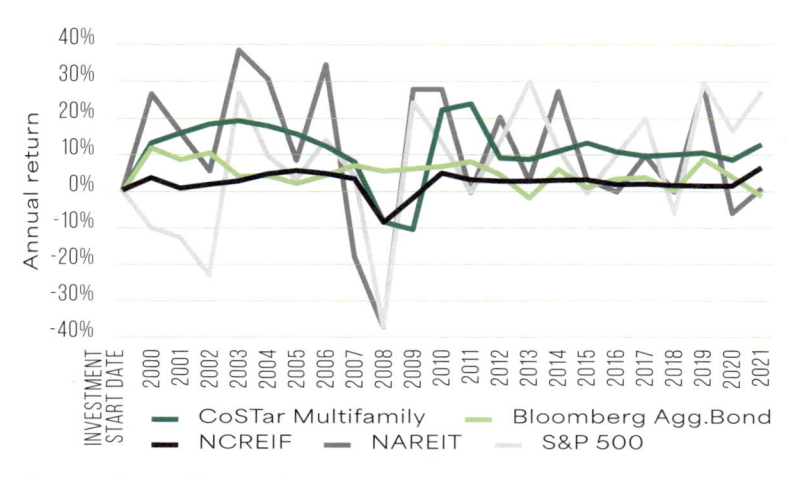

Source: Roers Companies

The second chart below shows the performance of a $10,000 investment since the year 2000. It shows that multifamily real estate has outperformed the other asset classes.

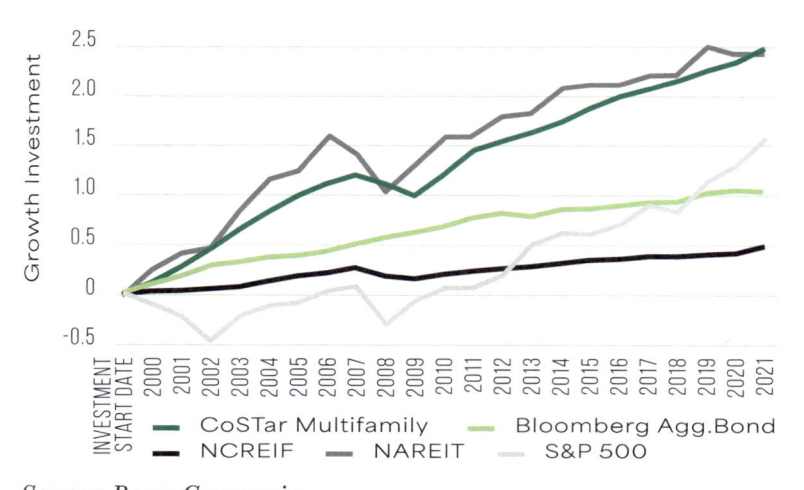

Source: Roers Companies

When I began to research passive real estate syndication investing, I was looking for something different. I wanted to reduce my dependence upon the W2, ditch traditional Wall Street investing, and retire with more time to call my own.

I also did not want to invest in something that required my time. I now had four children, two of whom were recently adopted, and a busy job. So, I was already spread too thinly. Nor did I want to get back into actively managing properties.

"Why don't you park your money in real estate syndications?" a friend asked me.

My friend was already investing in syndications, I knew he was enjoying it, and I wanted to know more.

He put me in touch with the main sponsor of the group he invested in, and I reached out to him. I did not know what questions to ask, so he gave me the pitch deck, so to speak.

I trusted my friend who had a great track record with this sponsor. But, apart from that, I am ashamed to say, I used the shotgun approach. I held my breath and plugged my nose. I deployed capital into the deal without knowing what was going to happen next. I do not advise that as a strategy.

I was lucky. That first investment started producing regular, consistent distributions of between seven to nine percent on an annualized basis. After four years, the property sold, and I got my original capital back. I had basically doubled my money. I was receiving six to eight percent in annualized cash distributions paid to me as an investor on a quarterly basis. Plus, at the end of the four-year term, there

> **LIMITED PARTNER (LP):** A passive investor in a real estate syndication who contributes capital to the investment but has limited involvement in the decision-making and management of the property. Limited partners typically benefit from potential returns and tax advantages without active participation.

> **GENERAL PARTNER (GP):** The syndicator or sponsor who takes an active role in managing the real estate investment. General partners often have more significant responsibilities and contribute their expertise and experience to ensure the success of the project.

was a pool of money left over, which was profit. That cash was split between the LIMITED PARTNER (LP) investors, which included me, and the GENERAL PARTNER (GP) who was the sponsor of the syndication team running the VALUE-ADD business plan.

I was hooked.

As I said, I was lucky, and I am much more careful now when I select deals and sponsors. Today, I am a fund manager for my company, Starting Point Capital. I also host a podcast on real estate syndication called *The Freedom Point Podcast*. On that podcast, I challenge sponsors because now I know the types of questions to ask people in this space. Sometimes listeners call me and say, "You were kind of rough on that guy," but, the truth is, I know the pitfalls. There are people who are wolves in sheep's clothing who will overpromise and underdeliver.

"Jeremy, I've got somebody that's got this great investment opportunity," people often tell me. "It's a multifamily real estate value-add, and the sponsor's projecting an 18 percent internal RATE OF RETURN. But every opportunity you've told me about has a return of 16 or 17 percent. So, what's going on here?"

The reality is that you should not be investing in a shiny pitch deck that makes lofty promises. Forget that I am a hypocrite and that I did. I fell for the glossy PDF that showed an impressive return. I knew there were no guarantees, and that there was risk, but I also knew that the risk comes back to the sponsor of the project. I considered how the sponsor planned to de-risk the opportunity. I was lucky in a way, but I was also willing to take on the risk to really find out what real estate syndication was all about. To some extent, you only learn by doing.

As I said, I was so taken with real estate syndication that I started my own private equity company, Starting Point Capital. But, I should say that, what I was so taken with was the project operators and their effectiveness or lack thereof. Before I explain more about my initial experiences with real estate syndication, let us take a broad look at the value of real estate as an investment vehicle because it is important

> **VALUE-ADD:** A strategy in real estate where investors seek out properties that have the potential for increased income through renovations, re-branding, or improvements in management.

> **RATE OF RETURN:** The gain or loss on an investment over a specified period expressed as a percentage of the investment's cost.

to understand how it works compared to other alternative investments.

THE KINETICS OF CASH FLOW

During the global financial crisis of 2008, my mother suggested that I invest in precious metals—gold, silver, and platinum—or commodities like oil and gas. These investments were supposed to tame the inflation monster because Wall Street was struggling. She was right in that commodities are hard assets, but there is no guarantee of future value. Now, I am all for diversification, but I do not remember anyone suggesting investing in a hard asset to produce cash flow. Last time I checked, if you own a commodity or precious metal, those assets do not produce consistent cash flow with tax benefits.

Your gold bars are doing nothing for you. You hope they will appreciate in value, but there is no guarantee. If you look at the price of gold or silver, for example, from 2008 until today, the return barely exceeds the rate of inflation over that 30-plus-year period. That is not a hedge against inflation or, at least, it is not one that works.

Now, let us look at savings bonds backed by the United States government. Bonds are often considered good investments when the stock market is not performing. Your Series EE or I Series bonds are probably averaging three to four percent in a good year but, if inflation is anywhere from two to ten percent, then you are either maintaining the status quo or your purchasing power is slowly deteriorating over time.

Why is cash flow so important?

Wealth preservation is a concern for many investors and rightly so. The trick is to leverage the velocity of money. When money sits, it loses value. When we accelerate money and turn it over, cash flow increases, and that turnover really starts to work for you. That is why investors invest passively into value-add real estate deals where the asset will often be sold for a higher value, and they then reinvest over and over and compound their wealth.

With passive real estate investing, a popular strategy is to invest into value-add properties that have an expected hold period of two to five years, dispose of the property, and then reinvest into the next value-add project. You can then recycle any capital and keep it moving in the system. CDs, gold, stocks, and savings bonds are good for diversification but, if you are looking to grow your wealth versus just to preserve your wealth, then you need investments that produce regular consistent cash flow and allow you to turn that money over kinetically.

Your 401(k) is an example of an asset that is not kinetic. A couple of years ago, I ran a quick and dirty exercise where I compared the return from my 401(k) to the return from my passive real estate investing over a 20-year period. I looked at the amount of personal money I had invested in my 401(k) regardless of the company match and regardless of the actual performance over the course of that period. I compared that amount to the amount of money that I put into passive real estate investing regardless of the cash flow distributions that I regularly receive on those investments.

I calculated what the expected profit split would be at the end of that cycle. I found that, if I had taken the money that I had put into my 401(k) over a 20-year period and invested it passively into a real estate syndication instead, my investments would have performed twice as well. This includes my company match, which is free money and pre-tax. I should add here that your 401(k) balance may be somewhat of a facade as you have not yet paid taxes on the market appreciation. The gains are tax-deferred instead of tax-exempt. That $1,000,000 balance will become something less once you start taking distributions in retirement.

Another reason rich people invest in real estate is the tax DEPRECIATION benefit. My 401(k) is a pre-tax investment. With passive real estate investing, I am not paying taxes on my regular distributions received. It is not a pre-tax investment, but any capital contributions that I make to this investment are largely growing tax-free.

DEPRECIATION: An accounting method of allocating the cost of a tangible asset over its useful life. In real estate, it allows investors to deduct the costs from their taxes, reflecting the property's decrease in value over time.

Why? Because of the IRS rules around depreciation and how investors are able to use passive paper loss depreciation on these investments to reduce or eliminate future capital gains.

THE TAX BENEFITS OF PASSIVE INVESTING IN REAL ESTATE

Unlike when you invest in stocks and mutual funds, investing in real estate can lower the amount of taxes you owe even while you are making great returns on your investment. The IRS views real estate gains differently from other types of gains.

But, first, here is a disclaimer.

I am not a tax professional, nor will I ever seek to become one (those people have really tough jobs). As such, the insights and perspectives I offer come from my experience only. You should speak with your CPA for more details and for specifics on your situation.

OK, now that that is out of the way, let us dive in.

There are seven things you should know about taxes and passive investing in a real estate syndication:

1. THE TAX CODE FAVORS REAL ESTATE INVESTORS.

The IRS recognizes that real estate investing provides quality housing that is needed in many urban and rural areas. As such, the tax code is written in a way that rewards real estate investing, maintaining units, and making upgrades over time (more on these benefits in a moment). So, as a real estate investor, you are like the IRS's doormat, and that comes with benefits.

2. AS A PASSIVE INVESTOR, YOU GET ALL THE TAX BENEFITS AN ACTIVE INVESTOR GETS.

Even though you are not actively fixing any toilets, evicting tenants, or climbing on any roofs, you still get the full tax benefits of the active investor. This is because, as a passive investor in a real estate syndication, you invest in an entity (typically, a limited liability company (LLC) or limited partner (LP)) that owns the property, and that entity is disregarded in the eyes of the IRS (these entities are called "pass-through entities"). That means that any tax benefits flow right through that entity to you, the investor.

Note: This does not apply if you invest in REAL ESTATE INVESTMENT TRUSTS (REITs). With a REIT, you are investing in a publicly traded entity, not directly in the underlying real estate, and hence you do not get the same tax benefits.

Common tax benefits from investing in real estate include writing off expenses related to the

---

REAL ESTATE INVESTMENT TRUST (REIT):
A company that owns, operates, or finances income-producing real estate. REITs offer a way for investors to receive a share of the income produced through commercial real estate ownership without actually having to buy, manage, or finance any properties themselves.

property (including things like repairs, utilities, payroll, and interest) and writing off the value of the property over time (depreciation).

3. DEPRECIATION IS POWERFUL.

Depreciation is one of the most powerful wealth-building tools in real estate. Period. The IRS uses depreciation to acknowledge a decrease in value of an asset over time from wear and tear. Depreciation is then used as an expense that investors can count against their income. The IRS uses a 27.5-year period when determining the time frame in which residential real estate assets wear down and 39 years for commercial real estate. Depreciation is not unique to real estate, but real estate investing uniquely benefits from depreciation.

For example, a $20 million multifamily property (with $5 million raised from passive investors) depreciated over 39 years provides a tax shelter to the investors of $512,820 per year ($20 million/39 years). If you invested $100,000 passively into this property, then you would receive two percent ($100,000/$5 million) of the total depreciation benefit, which equates to $10,256 per year. Assuming a tax rate of 20 percent, your potential tax savings would be $2,051 per year. Note that this does not include accelerated depreciation through a cost segregation study (which we use on our investment properties) or bonus depreciation, which will be discussed later.

Additionally, you can activate your passive depreciation losses in the same year to offset gains on your investment distributions if you are a real estate professional. Among other requirements, to qualify as a real estate professional, the IRS requires you to spend 750 hours or more on active real estate activities. However, even if you do not qualify as a real estate professional, eventually you can activate your passive depreciation loss activity at the time of deposition (when the real estate property is sold). The suspended accumulated depreciation can be used to offset the profit split you receive in the year of a property sale.

Keep in mind that, when you exit a passive real estate opportunity, you will likely have to recapture the depreciation and pay taxes on the tax recapture. This dynamic creates an incentive to use a 1031 exchange strategy (see number 6). The 1031 allows you to pay no taxes on your gains by "trading" into another real estate property as you "rollover" your capital and profit into the next real estate opportunity.

The Tax Cuts and Jobs Act of 2017 adjusted the existing tax law to allow an incentive for investors to deduct up to and sometimes exceeding 100 percent of the depreciation expenses in the first year of ownership versus deducting over a five, seven, or 15-year depreciation period. This provides a unique opportunity for the passive investor to take advantage of accelerated passive losses in the first year they invest in a property through the syndication model. Imagine what this looks like when investing passively in a single $20 million commercial real estate syndication!

At the time of this writing, the bonus depreciation has been slowly phasing out each year and, unless the United States Congress acts, bonus depreciation will phase out completely in the next few years. That said, depreciation benefits will still have an effect, just not as much as they will accelerate in the first years of the investment.

4. COST SEGREGATION IS DEPRECIATION ON STEROIDS.

Straight-line depreciation allows you to write off an equal amount of the value of the asset every year for 27.5 years. However, for a typical real estate syndication, the hold time is around five years. So, if we were to deduct an equal amount every year for 27.5 years, we would only get five years of those benefits. We would be leaving the remaining 22.5 years of depreciation benefits on the table. This is where cost segregation comes in.

COST SEGREGATION acknowledges the fact that not every asset in the property is created equally. For example, the printer in the back office has a much shorter lifespan than the roof on top of the building.

> **COST SEGREGATION:** A tax strategy used to accelerate depreciation on certain components of a property, allowing investors to reduce their taxable income more quickly. It involves a detailed engineering analysis of the property to identify and reclassify assets into shorter depreciation schedulesrather than the standard depreciation timeline for real estate.

Under current depreciation rules, the modified accelerated cost recovery system (MACRS) depreciates a newly acquired or constructed building over 39 years on a straight-line basis (27.5 years for apartments). Under certain circumstances, MACRS allows for the reallocation of a portion of the property into asset categories having shorter depreciable lives (e.g., five, seven, and 15 years).

A cost segregation study can shift property (and the associated dollars) from categories that have long tax lives to categories that have shorter tax lives. This allows for greater depreciation during the early years of the asset's life, thereby lowering taxable income and thus lowering taxes. The result of the accelerated depreciation is improved cash flow to the property owner.

In a cost segregation study, an engineer itemizes the individual components that make up a property, including things like outlets, wiring, windows, carpeting, and fixtures.

Certain items can be depreciated on a shorter timeline—five, seven, or 15 years—instead of over 27.5 years. This can drastically increase the depreciation benefits in those early years.

A cost segregation study allows you to break the asset down into different components and depreciate them according to the actual rate in which materials depreciate. For example, carpet might depreciate over a five-year time frame while appliances might depreciate over seven years. To leverage this strategy, a third-party cost segregation specialist must be contracted to perform an engineering study of the property.

Here is an example based upon a true story.

A few years ago, a real estate syndication group purchased an apartment building in December. That meant that the investors only held that asset for one month of that calendar year. However, due largely to cost segregation, the depreciation schedule was accelerated for many items that were part of the property, including things like appliances and carpeting.

The SCHEDULE K-1 form that was sent out to investors the following spring showed that, if you had invested $100,000 in that real estate syndication, you showed a paper loss of $50,000. That is 50 percent of the original investment just for having invested into the property for a single month during that tax year.

If you or your spouse qualify as a real estate professional, that paper loss can apply to the rest of your taxes, including any taxes you owe based upon your salary, side hustle, or other investment gains.

SCHEDULE K-1: Schedule K-1 is an Internal Revenue Service (IRS) tax form issued annually. It reports the gains, losses, interest, dividends, earnings, and other distributions from certain investments or business entities for the previous tax year. The K-1 form reports each participant's share of the business entity's gains, losses, deductions, credits, and other distributions (whether or not they are actually distributed).

Unless you qualify as a real estate professional, you can only use passive paper depreciation loss to offset passive income. But, if I am investing in real estate passively, every time I make an investment in year one, I will historically get a 40 to 60 percent passive paper depreciation loss. So, if I invest $100,000 into a passive real estate opportunity, in year one on my K-1 at the end of the year, I will have a $40,000 to $60,000 passive paper loss. However, I cannot use that depreciation loss to offset my active income unless my wife or I can qualify as a real estate professional.

If neither my spouse nor I can claim that designation, it does not mean that we lose the depreciation benefit. It just gets suspended or carried forward into another year when I might have a passive gain through distributions or the **EQUITY PROFIT SPLIT** once the deal goes full cycle. At that point, I can activate that depreciation to offset the capital gains taxes on the money that I have received from my passive investment.

Now, if my spouse or I can claim real estate professional status, we can then use passive paper depreciation loss activity to offset any active income. In our case, Marlene qualified as a real estate professional because of the

---

EQUITY PROFIT SPLIT: Also known as the "promote," the equity profit split describes how the profits from an opportunity are to be distributed among the limited partners and the general partner (sponsor). For example, in an 85-15 split, the limited partners will get 85 percent of the profits, and the general partner or sponsor will receive 15 percent.

active managing support she was providing to my company, Starting Point Capital. Because of that, our federal tax bracket went from 37 percent to 12 percent.

The tax benefit that real estate status brings is so significant that I have had investors restructure their lives. In a case where one spouse is the breadwinner making six figures per year and the other spouse is working part-time, it often makes sense for the spouse earning less to get their real estate license or actively manage a real estate property. They can spend 750 hours per year on active real estate activities to reduce the amount of taxes the higher earner pays on their W2. With their collective investments in passive real estate, they can use the passive depreciation loss activities in the same year against the spouse's active ordinary income.

5. CAPITAL GAINS AND DEPRECIATION RECAPTURE ARE THINGS FOR WHICH YOU SHOULD PLAN.

Of course, real estate investing is not 100 percent tax-free. The IRS gets their cut through capital gains taxes when a real estate asset is sold and, sometimes, through DEPRECIATION RECAPTURE, depending upon the sale price.

> **DEPRECIATION RECAPTURE:** The gain realized by the sale of depreciable capital property. Gains must be reported as ordinary income for tax purposes. Depreciation recapture is assessed when the sale price of an asset exceeds the tax basis or adjusted cost basis. The difference between these figures is "recaptured" when it is reported as ordinary income.

In a real estate syndication that holds a property for five years, you would not have to worry about capital gains taxes and depreciation recapture until the asset is sold in year five. The specific amount of capital gains and depreciation recapture depends upon the length of the hold time as well as your individual tax bracket.

6. 1031 EXCHANGES ARE AMAZING.

When a real estate asset is sold, the investor owes capital gains taxes (and, often, depreciation recapture). However, there is one way around this. And that is through a 1031 exchange.

> **1031 EXCHANGE:** A swap of one real estate investment property for another that allows capital gains taxes to be deferred.

A 1031 EXCHANGE allows you to sell one investment property and, within a set amount of time, swap that asset for another similar investment property. If you do exchange the asset within the IRS-required time frame, instead of having the profits paid out directly to you, you can roll them into the next investment. Then, you do not owe any capital gains when the first property is sold as the burden has effectively been "deferred" onto the next investment property. This strategy can then be repeated over and over, thus deferring tax consequences indefinitely. You are now effectively using the IRS's money at a zero-percent loan to produce an accelerated return profile.

Only some real estate syndications offer a 1031 exchange as an option. Sometimes, the majority of the investors in a syndication have to agree to a 1031 exchange to make it a possibility. Unfortunately, you cannot always execute a 1031 exchange. Why? Because the SPONSOR must agree to allow you to bring 1031 exchange money into the deal, there has to be room left in the opportunity, and you must meet certain required time frames.

There is also a LAZY 1031, which is an investment strategy that investors can use if they cannot participate in a 1031 exchange.

Let us say that I am a limited partner exiting an investment. I have been paid my preferred rate of return, and I have some profit. So, I have doubled my money in three to five years. It would be nice if I did not have to pay capital gains taxes on the profit from Property A when that deal goes full cycle. With a lazy 1031 exchange, I can take my original capital, profit from Property A,

SPONSOR: The general partners or operators responsible for sourcing, evaluating, and managing the real estate investment on behalf of the passive investors. The syndicator/sponsor takes the lead in identifying opportunities, negotiating deals, and overseeing the operations of the investment.

LAZY 1031: A provision in the IRS code allowing investors to continue to defer capital gains taxes on the exchange of like-kind properties, usually in the case of large sums of money and high net worth individuals.

and invest it in a different but similar investment property, Property B, in the same calendar year.

Property B is also going to have depreciation and, as long as Property B produces depreciation loss activity, I can use that depreciation loss on my K-1 to offset the tax consequences on Property A that I rolled out of in that same year. If you cannot use all of the passive depreciation losses in the current tax year, they can be suspended into future years, indefinitely.

The 1031 exchange differs from the lazy 1031 exchange mainly because it typically involves larger sums of money. For example, it might be used in the case of a high net worth individual with an investment of $500,000 or a million dollars who wants to 1031 exchange that into the next deal and continue to perform a 1031 exchange indefinitely.

They might choose to execute a 1031 because their basis continues to drop. And, as the basis in that investment continues to drop, because they are using depreciation as a tax advantage strategy, eventually, when they decide to pull that money off the table and not reinvest it, depreciation recapture comes into play. There is no depreciation recapture if they continue to defer or continue to reinvest that capital through a 1031 exchange strategy. When a wealthy person who continued to execute a 1031 strategy dies, their basis gets reset, and their heirs never have to pay the piper: the IRS.

7. SOME PEOPLE INVEST IN REAL ESTATE SOLELY FOR THE TAX BENEFITS.

The tax benefits of investing in real estate are so powerful that some people do so purely to take advantage of the tax benefits, and that is what keeps me reinvesting. You see, by investing in real estate, people can leverage significant write-offs and then apply those to the other taxes they owe, thereby decreasing their overall tax bill.

This is how real estate tycoons can make millions of dollars but owe next to nothing in taxes.

It is perfectly legal, and it is a powerful wealth-building strategy. Moreover, you do not have to be wealthy to take advantage of the tax benefits of investing in real estate. The tax code makes the benefits of investing in real estate applicable to every real estate investor.

As a passive investor, you do not have to actually do anything to take advantage of the tax benefits that come with investing in real estate. That is one of the benefits of being a passive investor. You do not have to keep any receipts or itemize repairs. You just get that K-1 every year, hand it over to your accountant, and that is it. It is just that good.

Allow me to get a little philosophical for a moment. I am sure that everyone has their own personal experiences that are impossible to compartmentalize and separate from their professional and financial lives. Our psychological states and the decisions we make are the result of what is going on and has gone on in our lives.

When I was searching for another way to use my time and my money, I was trying to satisfy a value that I held. I have always followed a faith-based path in life, and the daily grind left little time to pursue quality family time or be involved in our community.

When we were college students, Marlene and I had spent time teaching English to university students in Mongolia. It was a time of profound realization for us both. We were in a small town called Zuunmod, which is so remote that it feels as though it literally is at the end of the Earth. Life was slow, and there were few resources. I would not describe the people as living in poverty because they had what they needed. In fact, it seemed that they had more than rich Westerners do. I realized how much stress we, as Westerners, experience because we never enjoy the simple things in life like a conversation with a neighbor, playing a game with a child, or a few minutes gazing at the landscape. What I took away from that trip was a sense of community. I also wanted to find more time to play a role in that community wherever it may be.

THE CASE FOR PASSIVE INVESTING

For many professionals, the idea of becoming a real estate investor is appealing. The allure of creating passive income streams and building wealth through property is strong.

However, for those with demanding careers and a family, actively managing real estate investments can be a time-consuming and stressful endeavor. Instead, a more effective strategy for busy professionals is to invest passively in real estate and focus on excelling in their W2 jobs.

As a busy professional, your time is your most valuable asset. Actively managing real estate involves a myriad of tasks—from property acquisition, tenant management, and maintenance to dealing with unexpected issues that arise. This can quickly become overwhelming, especially when balancing a full-time job. Passive investing allows you to put your money to work without requiring significant time commitments, enabling you to focus on advancing your career.

Passive real estate investing allows you to leverage the expertise of experienced operators and sponsors. These professionals have the knowledge and resources to identify profitable opportunities, manage properties efficiently, and navigate the complexities of real estate markets. By investing with seasoned professionals, you benefit from their experience while avoiding the steep learning curve and potential pitfalls of active investing.

Passive real estate investments, such as real estate syndications, offer diversification across various markets, property types, and geographical locations. This diversification reduces risk and provides a more stable income stream. Achieving this level of diversification as an active investor would require substantial time, capital, and effort, which most busy professionals simply do not have.

Your W2 job likely offers you a steady income, career growth, and benefits that are difficult to match through real estate—at least initially. By focusing on your career, you can maximize your earning potential, enhance your lifestyle, and increase your savings capacity. This, in turn, provides you with more capital to invest passively, accelerating your wealth-building journey.

Active real estate investing comes with significant responsibilities and risks. Market fluctuations, tenant issues, legal challenges, and property damage are just a few of the headaches that active investors must manage. Passive investing shifts these burdens to experienced operators, allowing you to enjoy the financial benefits of real estate without the associated stress and risk.

Passive real estate investing is a powerful tool for long-term wealth building. It provides consistent cash flow, appreciation potential, and tax benefits while requiring minimal effort on your part. Over time, your passive investments can grow significantly, complementing your W2 income and setting you up for a financially secure retirement.

I became convinced that passive real estate investing was right for me, and it could be right for many others. There were clearly so many benefits. And, once I saw the proof in the pudding, so to speak, I decided to create my own private equity company, Starting Point Capital.

III
THE NEW BUILD: STARTING POINT CAPITAL

I have always had a bit of a daredevil streak in me. Whether it is taking on a new challenge, exploring uncharted territory, or diving into something that others might shy away from, I find excitement in pushing the limits. This mindset is not just about seeking thrills—it has been a key driver in my high-performance sales career. I have never been content with just meeting expectations; I push to exceed them, exploring innovative strategies and taking calculated risks that others might avoid.

This same daredevil approach carries over into how I invest. I am drawn to opportunities that require bold moves and clear vision where the potential rewards match the level of risk. I believe that calculated risk, coupled with a strong strategy, is essential in both business and investing. Life is too short to play it safe all the time, and that is where the real growth happens—

when you are willing to step out of your comfort zone and chase after what others might see as too daring.

The next stage of my life brought profound change. I would be lying if I said that the sequence of events occurred organically. They did not. I forced them because I had a vision of what I wanted my life to be like, and I was impatient to get there.

As is always the case, life threw us a few curve balls. After our second son was born, Marlene had her tubes tied. Three years later, we regretted that decision and attempted to have the procedure reversed. That failed so, in 2015, we looked into adopting both locally in Minnesota and internationally.

As I mentioned before, Marlene and I had visited Mongolia and China before we married when we taught English there. We were drawn to the people and the culture of that region. We were also friends with another couple who had adopted a Chinese child so, after many discussions with them, we were comfortable with the decision to do the same. We hired an adoption agency.

Although we were seeking to adopt a little girl, we knew that we did not want to close any doors along the way. We were approved to adopt a girl, a boy, or even siblings if the opportunity came along. After a long adoption process, we were matched with a set of twins. Our long-term goal was to eventually adopt two children so, when twins were presented, we doubled down and took the leap with two at once. We have never regretted it for a second, and we firmly believe that these two are a perfect fit for our family.

The experience was profound and all-consuming. It was impossible to imagine how life-changing it would be to integrate two new people from a different culture, who did not know our language nor we theirs, into our family and way of life. Everyone was affected, everyone had a new role, and everyone struggled.

What the experience impressed upon me was the value of time. Like many, I have a difficult time with work-life balance. Turning the work switch off is one of my greatest weaknesses. It is particularly difficult today when we are connected to emails and instant messages and are expected to field customer calls 24/7.

Our decision to adopt the twins made me determined to find a way to live that part of my life the right way, with quality, and not be all-consumed with work and finances. It was time to stop and learn new ways to create income streams that did not require more of my time. I was looking for passive income streams that released our dependence upon chasing future paychecks.

UNLOCKING FUTURE PAYCHECK DEPENDENCE

I started Starting Point Capital when I realized that, through passive investing in real estate syndication, I could escape the trappings of Wall Street, invest in real estate, and not have to swing hammers. I got all the benefits with none of the headaches, and I could reduce my dependence upon my W2. Best of all, I could apply my passion for networking and sales background to raise capital for best-in-class syndicators.

Passive investing in real estate was also the path of least resistance. What I mean by that: I was noticing the effects of diminishing returns in my day job. I could spend 50 percent more time on my corporate job with limited upside results and getting more exhausted in the process.

We all only have so many hours in a day and so many days in a week. The challenge is that most people in the professional world are spending an enormous amount of time on things that do not matter, resulting in so much wasted time. Back in the day, we used to call them water cooler conversations. Today, it could be scrolling on LinkedIn or having banal conversations with colleagues that do not lead to further productivity or future results. It could be having a mental pity party in our head because something did not go our way when we lost a sale.

The point is that there is a way to produce the same volume of productivity while giving less of your time. That is the theory behind passive investing. The velocity of money and the power behind it produces greater results than spending your time doing something else. It is a way to optimize your investing and your time.

When I first invested in a passive real estate opportunity, a friend suggested I put money into a debt equity fund. He explained the deal structure and, if the investment delivered what it promised, it could be just the type of thing I was looking for. The concept of passive investing was one I could follow and make sense of because I could see how I could get results without putting in more time and effort. There would be no diminishing returns.

Later, when I had more deals under my belt and was fully sold on real estate syndications, I realized that finding the path of least resistance meant tapping into my deep network of people who know me personally and professionally. My network could then be used to leverage the creation of my own private equity firm. That network included family, friends, current and former sales colleagues, small business owners, and franchise consultants.

NETWORKS AND FRANCHISEES

At ADP, I was regularly critiqued for doing things outside of the guardrails and often found myself in a position of having to beg for forgiveness later. I knew that ADP's sales strategy was designed for the average performer, but that was not me. I knew that my way was going to lead to exceptional performance.

My path of least resistance was to focus upon the relationships I built. In my early days at ADP, it was picking up the phone, knocking on doors, and buying donuts at the local bakery to deliver them to clients on a Friday in exchange for a scheduled appointment the following week.

Later, I used the network of relationships I had built from my early days in banking to secure leads. I spoke the lingo, after all. Because of my contacts, there was less need to knock on doors or cold-call small business owners. Leveraging those relationships gave me access to the franchising space, which led to a huge transformation in ADP's sales.

ADP had no formal relationships with any franchise brands before I came along. I am talking about the brands you can find now at virtually any commercial retail center in North America. Think of Dairy Queen, Anytime Fitness, and Great Clips. If ADP could supply any such franchise with human capital management solutions, that would be a huge market grab for the company. If I could convince the franchise to partner with ADP, I could have access to all of their small business franchise owners across the system.

I managed to secure a Dairy Queen franchise, and then another, and then I used those sales as leverage for an introduction to the corporate franchisor. It was easy to convince the corporate franchisor to use ADP as their preferred vendor. Once we were already working with a few of their franchise owners, it was simply a matter of making it official. I now had access to 4,500 Dairy Queen locations across the country, and I had the support and endorsement of the franchisor.

Fast forward to today, and ADP has a whole team dedicated to this strategy called the franchise program. We have several-hundred relationships with franchise brands—anywhere from big brands to baby brands. I was the pioneer in that effort and was given the opportunity to help create the foundation and vision for the future.

Accessing franchisees was a huge step for me and for ADP. It opened up a network of entrepreneurs that I could later tap into when I was seeking to partner with investors on future passive real estate investment opportunities. Most franchisees realize the need to generate supplemental income, passive income, or additional streams of income. That is why they sought out a franchise in the first place. Now, a good part of my network of investors for real estate syndication opportunities are franchisees, franchise consultants, or franchise suppliers who want to partner with us, diversify, and create additional streams of income.

I have learned a lot in the 20 years I have been working with franchisees, including how most of them are in the same position that I was. They want to replace their dependence upon the W2. They do not want to spend the rest of their years working to fulfill somebody else's dreams. Also, many of them are distrustful of Wall Street investing. They are turning to investments that they can have more control over, which is often Main Street.

FIRST INVESTMENTS

After continuing my education by consuming books, listening to podcasts, networking with industry experts, and doing my own research into real estate syndications, I began investing. I received a six percent cash-on-cash return and an eight percent preferred return and expected equity upside (profit) when the sponsor sells the property in the future. Think of a high-YIELD savings or money market account. These returns are crazy when you consider that the best you could do with a money market account at the time was a 0.5 percent return, and the volatility of the market is often too great to bear.

> **YIELD:** The income return on an investment such as the interest or dividends received from holding a particular security. In real estate, it is often referred to as the yield on cost or the current yield.

After seeing what passive real estate could do, I was energized. I started exploring all aspects of real estate investing, including the debt side, equity side, syndication model, limited partner aspect, and the general partner role. Everything indicated that I could make a significantly better return than I could with a money market savings account or index funds.

Part of the reason I was so struck by real estate syndications was that I was investing directly with a team. The team was responsible for identifying, planning, and executing the project to produce the projected returns. My property flipping days had taught me that those returns are merely projections because it always comes down to the sponsor's ability to execute the business plan.

Apart from the appeal of passive income from real estate, I also appreciated that, as an investor, I could pick up the phone and talk to the guy who was calling the shots. My investment gave me a stake in the company that owned the specific property, and I could hop on the phone with the general partner or the sponsor any time and get an update. You cannot do that when you are investing in Wall Street. I cannot pick up the phone, call Elon Musk, and say, "Elon, hey, what are your plans for SpaceX?"

After that one investment in 2015, we doubled our money by 2019. We did not make any additional real estate investments as a passive investment during that four-year period. I wanted the strategy to prove itself out.

When we saw the results in 2019, we went crazy. From 2019 to 2024, we invested in 29 more projects.

Our first project was a multifamily project, but we have since diversified into retail, assisted living, and flex office projects. There are plenty of other real estate **PROPERTY CLASSES** and projects to invest in outside of B-class multi-family apartments.

PROPERTY CLASS: Categories used to describe the quality and location of a property. Common classes are A (luxury), B (mid-grade workforce housing), and C (affordable or older).

In 2022, we had 15 projects, and I was so excited about real estate syndication that I started spreading the gospel. I was telling friends, family, colleagues, neighbors, and customers.

"Guys," I was saying. "This is mind-blowing."

"OK," they said. "Show us."

So, I did, by building Starting Point Capital.

INVESTING WITH STARTING POINT CAPITAL

A real estate syndication is a deal structure between a sponsor and various investors. The investors are passive, meaning that they do not do any property development or management, and the sponsor (or general partner) is responsible for buying the target property, implementing the value-add or renovating it and, ultimately, selling the property if that is in the business plan. The investors receive a portion of the operating profits and a split of the profits when the property is sold.

My role at Starting Point Capital is to educate investors on the benefits of passive real estate investing and build a community of investors that partner with us on future real estate syndication opportunities. I build relationships with the investors that provide much of the capital for the sponsor.

The process begins when I receive the business plan from a sponsor. That is where my time with ADP proved to be so useful.

I have a vast network and a playbook to back it up. I can also assess a sponsor and know what to look for in terms of red flags.

A key point is that I am investing along with the limited partners in the project. Because I am investing in the project, too, and walking the walk with them, that gives our investors' confidence because, if I trust the sponsor, so can they.

If the sponsor and the business plan pass our strict due diligence, I begin notifying my investor network that a future investment opportunity is on the horizon. Typically, I have worked with the sponsor on investments in the past, so there is a level of trust between us. It is on me to gain the trust of the investors, but I usually have a relationship with them, too.

"Have you done this type of investing before?" I am often asked by investors.

"Yes," I tell them. "Thirty times. And I'm not stopping."

My enthusiasm is clear. I will explain how the investments work and the compounding. I share how, when I exit out of a property, I put my capital into the next one and then the next. However, I am not putting in $50,000 as the newbie investor might be. I am putting in six figures or more because my investment doubled over the past investment hold period, and I am redeploying the original capital and profit earned.

"You're really good at this," Todd Dexheimer, co-founder and principal at Endurus Capital said to me a couple of years ago. He was talking about finding limited partner investors.

"For the next opportunity that we have, why don't you bring your network together, and you guys invest in the opportunity? In exchange for the collective capital you raise, we'll give your investors a better projected return profile."

We had already discussed the project terms, but this meant that I could now monetize my network. So, we structured the deal as a fund of funds where our collective group of investors pooled our dollars together to deploy directly into the sponsor's opportunity. That meant I could receive a split on the profit that the deal was projected to produce when it would go full cycle.

In a nutshell, that was how Starting Point Capital was launched. I secured a website domain name, hired a graphics designer to create a logo, and presented that first opportunity, a value-add multifamily property, to investors. This was in 2022, and I had no idea what to expect.

I raised a million dollars on that deal, and I could have raised more. The challenge was that it filled up so quickly. There is a point where we have to shut off the spigot. We can only raise so much money for these opportunities before we have to tell investors, "I'm sorry, but you missed out on this one."

That first deal filled up in 23 hours. The next day, my phone blew up.

"Hey Jeremy, I want to talk more about this real estate investment that you presented," said several in my personal and professional network.

"I'd love to talk to you about it," I said. "But, just so you know, you can't invest in it."

"Why not?"

"Because it's already filled up."

The year 2023 was a banner year for Starting Point Capital. We raised over $20 million from my professional network. We had hundreds of investors, and every deal that we raised investor capital on filled up, on average, in 48 hours.

It is almost a guarantee that, when an investor chooses to invest in one of our properties, they are going to tell three other people about it, and on it goes through word of mouth. The next section gives some examples of real estate syndication investments and, specifically, investments offered by Starting Point Capital.

STARTING POINT CAPITAL'S INVESTMENT BUY BOX

Starting Point Capital focuses mainly on multifamily properties in safe Class B and above neighborhoods. Think workforce housing where the majority of the population live. The interiors of these units tend to be classic and easy to upgrade. The opportunities are mainly in red states such as Arizona, Florida, Kentucky, North Carolina, Ohio, Tennessee, and Texas. Some of the opportunities are outside of the more favorable regulatory environment. Blue states sometimes put rent caps on the increase in rental prices, and there are other regulatory headwinds prevalent.

Starting Point Capital targets properties built in the 1980s and 1990s. They have the typical classic interiors of the period. Our business model is traditional value-add where the business plan is to completely rebrand the asset. The interiors are renovated with kitchens and bathrooms stripped down to the studs with new appliances, platinum finishes, new flooring, new cabinets, new vanities, two-tone paint, a new monument sign out front, and a new pool deck.

Starting Point Capital has not historically partnered with investors on traditional ground-up development. These are typically A class asset projects, including a luxury property community with little renovations or value-add. We also have not historically invested in C class and D class because these projects are difficult to manage and come with a greater amount of risk to the investor. The tenant base demographic can also be challenging.

We focus on B class, which is where the majority of our population lives today, and we force appreciation through a value-add business plan.

Value-add can be in the form of both operational value-add and physical value-add. Sometimes, the properties are in great shape, but their operations are terrible. This can be the case when the property management company is a third party.

The margins that these property management companies make are so slim that, for them to actually make money, they have to limit the resources spent on labor and, consequently, the level of expertise can be lower. When a property management company is subpar, often the building's occupancy is decreasing or, to maintain occupancy levels, the monthly rents are not keeping pace with the local market.

In that scenario, the sponsor could fire the property management company and bring in a new one, but that is a major disruption to the overall business operations, and it is expensive. If you can integrate property management with the overall business plan, you can manage your occupancy rates efficiently and avoid the cost of having to find new property management. This business structure is called vertically integrated property management, and it is the business model that Starting Point Capital most often supports. One of Starting Point Capital's main sponsors is Rise48 Equity. Rise48 has both a vertically integrated property management company called Rise48 Communities and a vertically integrated building construction company called Rise48 Construction.

VERTICAL VS. THIRD-PARTY PROPERTY MANAGEMENT

Property management is a critical factor that can make or break the success of an investment. When it comes to managing properties, syndicators generally have two options: Vertical (or vertically integrated) property management and third-party property management. Each approach has its own advantages, but I have found that vertically integrated property management offers distinct benefits that align better with my investment goals.

Vertical property management refers to a structure in which the syndication company owns and operates its own property management arm. In this model, the same team that acquires the property is also responsible for managing it day-to-day. This integration creates a seamless flow of information and decision-making as the management team is fully aligned with the syndicator's vision and objectives. In some cases, the vertically integrated property management entity goal is to simply break even as this division of the sponsor is largely an extension of the lead sponsor.

On the other hand, third-party property management involves hiring an external company to manage the property. This third-party firm typically has its own systems, processes, and priorities, which may not always perfectly align with the syndicator's goals. While this approach allows syndicators to leverage the expertise of a specialized property management firm, it also introduces a level of separation that can sometimes lead to misalignment or communication challenges.

One primary challenge with third-party property management occurs when they are not performing well. It can be a huge disruption to the overall business plan if the sponsor must replace a property management company versus replacing a few bad apple employees.

While third-party property management can be effective in certain situations, I prefer vertically integrated property management for its alignment of interests, enhanced communication, operational efficiency, and greater accountability. By keeping management in-house, I have increased confidence that the property is operating with the same care and attention that went into its acquisition. This approach not only helps to maximize returns but also provides peace of mind, knowing that the property is being managed by a team fully committed to its success.

STARTING POINT CAPITAL'S DEAL STRUCTURES

Real estate syndication investments rely upon the potential to increase rents, and it is not easy to make money with real estate syndication if you can only increase rents by around three percent per year. It is not unusual for a business plan to show the rent for a two-bedroom unit with one bath increasing from $1,200 to $1,650. That is a 37 percent increase, not a three percent increase year over year.

Government subsidies sometimes play a role in an opportunity, depending upon the market. In Texas, for example, there is a property tax abatement initiative. The idea is that the city or the county encourages sponsors to buy distressed properties, renovate them, and breathe life into those communities while also providing incentives for sponsors to set aside a number of units for lower-income families. There might be a project to renovate a property built 40 years ago. This can attract a different type of renter and a whole new community to a neighborhood.

Starting Point Capital plays a major role finding investors for real estate syndication operators. Operators, or sponsors, acquire properties worth $40, $50, or $60 million, and most sponsors that we partner with take low-leverage loans, typically 65-35 or 70-30. That means that they need to raise millions of dollars from limited partner passive investors to acquire a target asset. Sponsors in this space do not have $10 million in liquid cash—they are losing purchasing power if they do. That is why sponsors seek limited partner investors. Ultimately, the sponsor might need 250 limited partner investors, each investing $50,000 to $100,000, to acquire a target property.

Managing the relationships with 250 individual and unique investors takes a lot of person-power and administrative resources. The sponsor will struggle to take this on. Sure, they can take a one-to-many approach and send out monthly email updates on the project and the financials, but high net worth investors tend to demand a bit more transparency as well as a relationship with the key stakeholders, particularly when they are contributing $50,000 to $100,000 to a project.

Practically speaking, communicating at the individual investor level is costly and not viable for a sponsor to maintain a meaningful relationship with hundreds of investors. With Starting Point Capital, I am partnering with the sponsor and the investor, and I take care of the communication personally with those investors.

Why would an investor choose to go through Starting Point Capital when they could go directly to the sponsor as a retail investor? Well, I have mentioned the communication and transparency side of things, but there is also power in numbers.

When investors come through Starting Point Capital, they invest in a SPECIAL PURPOSE VEHICLE (SPV). Think of it as a fund of funds. That fund is basically a community of investors pooling their money to deploy into the same deal that a retail investor would go into. I am creating a single fund from a collective group of investors that will be deployed into the sponsor's deal. This creates a triple win.

As for the triple win, first, the sponsor benefits because they do not have to manage the communication with hundreds of investors. The second win is again a benefit to the sponsor,

> **SPECIAL PURPOSE VEHICLE (SPV):** A special purpose vehicle (SPV) in a fund of funds structure for a single asset is a legal entity created to pool capital from multiple investors and limit their liability to the extent of their investment in the SPV. The SPV's sole purpose is to invest in one particular asset, often directly into the lead sponsor's deal.

> **INTERNAL RATE OF RETURN (IRR):** A financial metric used to estimate the profitability of potential investments. It calculates an annualized rate of growth that an investment is expected to generate.

> **EQUITY MULTIPLE (EM):** A performance metric that measures the total return provided to investors. It is calculated by dividing the total cash distributions received from an investment by the total equity invested.

which is that I am bringing my family, friends, and professional network to the deal, saving them the trouble of having to fundraise themselves. Lastly, the third win is for investors, who get a better projected INTERNAL RATE OF RETURN (IRR) and EQUITY MULTIPLE (EM). Let me explain that.

A profit split occurs when these properties are sold or when there is a capital event such as a cash-out refinancing. When events like these occur, depending upon the deal structure, the limited partner investors might get 70 percent of all remaining profits, and the sponsor might receive 30 percent. This is part of the waterfall structure and will be outlined in the investment subscription documents. The senior lender is always paid first, then preferred equity, mezzanine debt, and common equity (limited partners). This is called the CAPITAL STACK.

The capital stack pays one tier of investors before it pays another in order of priority.

A WATERFALL STRUCTURE in real estate investing is a legal term used in a sponsor's OPERATING AGREEMENT.

The term defines how distributions and profits are paid, when the money is paid, and to whom the money is paid.

The cash flow from distributions and the profit split paid to investors at the time of a capital event (cash-out refinance or sale of property) are allocated to the general partner and limited partners according to the waterfall structure outlined in the sponsor's operating agreement.

A common example of a way the sponsor would craft a deal structure would be to offer an eight percent PREFERRED RETURN and then a 70-30 split on profits (paid to investors at the time of a capital event).

In this example, and after all operating expenses have been covered, passive investors should expect to receive an eight percent cash return on their investment. In most syndication deals, the CASH-ON-CASH RETURN and distributions are paid out to investors monthly or quarterly. In most value-add investment opportunities, the cash-on-cash returns are lower than

CAPITAL STACK: Represents the different types of financing used to purchase and maintain the investment property. It is typically structured from the most senior to the most junior in terms of repayment priority and includes senior debt, mezzanine debt, preferred equity, and common equity.

WATERFALL STRUCTURE: A method of distributing the cash flow from an investment that prioritizes different tiers of investors. Each tier must be fully paid in the sequence of distribution before moving on to the next tier.

OPERATING AGREEMENT: An arrangement among a company's members that outlines its business operations and the rights and responsibilities of its members.

PREFERRED RETURN: A priority return that must be paid to common equity investors before any distributions can be made to other types of equity holders.

CASH-ON-CASH RETURN: A rate of return that calculates the cash income earned on the cash invested in a property. Cash-on-cash return measures the annual return the investor made on the investment over the year.

the preferred investor return, because the property needs free flowing cash flow during the first couple of years in order to support the renovation efforts. Investors should expect the cash-on-cash returns to trend up over the course of the business plan. Any gap between the actual cash-on-cash return and the preferred return will accrue and will be caught up at the time of a sale.

After the preferred return bucket has been filled, remaining distributions and profit splits will be paid to the sponsor and limited partner according to the next waterfall bucket outlined in the operating agreement. In this example, the limited partner will receive a 70 percent split on remaining distributions and profits, and the sponsor will receive 30 percent.

To simplify this point, let us assume that, at the time of disposition (sale of asset), the property generates a $10 million profit. After the investment has returned 100% of the investors annual preferred return (in this example 8%), seventy percent of the profit will be paid to the limited partner and 30 percent will be paid to the general partner. The limited partner's share of profit is paid according to the percentage of equity ownership they have in the investment. When you passively invest in a real estate offering, you receive shares, and those acquired shares will determine your ownership level and how profits will be paid to investors when the deal goes full cycle.

Because of my relationship with the sponsor, I could negotiate a more favorable split in the waterfall. A retail investor might have additional splits with the sponsor if the deal over-performs. So, if the deal is in excess of a 15 percent IRR or 2x equity multiple, there is a 50-50 split.

In some cases, we leverage the additional split hurdle out of the deal. In most but not all cases, our investors with Starting Point Capital do not have that additional split in the waterfall and receive a better limited partner/sponsor split above the preferred return. So, a retail investor might receive a 70-30 split whereas, after the preferred return, our investors are getting an 85-15 split.

The projected IRR is another critical term to understand. The key component is to understand the difference between the deal level IRR and the net IRR projected to the limited partner investors.

The projected deal level IRR is the return based upon the cash inflow and outflow at the property level. While the deal level IRR may look good to a passive investor, it does not reflect the actual return that the investor expects to receive because it does not reflect sponsor fees and the waterfall structure.

The net IRR return to the limited partner investors reflects the actual projected return to the investor and factors in the profit split that the sponsor is proposing to take.

The IRR also incorporates the time value of money, which provides the investor with a more accurate depiction of the RETURN ON INVESTMENT (ROI).

> **RETURN ON INVESTMENT (ROI):** A measure used to evaluate the efficiency or profitability of an investment, calculated by dividing the net profit of the investment by the initial cost.

The underlying time value of money concept is simply the idea that a dollar today is worth more than a dollar tomorrow. This is true for three reasons: Inflation, the opportunity cost of another investment, and the risk associated with the low possibility that the dollar may not, in fact, be returned to the investor.

In the IRR calculation, the value of future money must be discounted. This is a concept that works similarly to compounded interest. The value of future money earned is linked to how a present dollar earns a return. This includes the idea that a distribution paid in later periods is paid on both that initial investment dollar and the distribution earned in earlier periods.

One drawback of the IRR calculation is that it assumes earlier cash distributions are reinvested at the same rate of return, which, depending upon the investor, may not be the case. That said, the IRR calculation is a good indicator of a real estate deal's overall rate of return.

We caution investors against chasing the highest IRR because a high IRR can sometimes mask significant risks or unrealistic assumptions in the investment. IRR is a time-sensitive metric, meaning shorter-term projects with quick returns can show higher IRR, even if the overall returns (cash flow or equity multiple) are lower.

Additionally, a high IRR may involve more speculative assumptions, such as aggressive rent growth, lower vacancy rates, or quicker sales timelines, which may not be achievable. Investors should focus on a balance of factors, including cash flow stability, risk profile, and long-term returns, rather than relying solely on IRR.

All that is to say that our investors are actually better off investing in a deal through Starting Point Capital because we have leverage with the sponsor that investors would not have going into the deal as a direct retail investor.

Let us use the Rise Sun Valley investment introduced at the beginning of the book as an example. Sun Valley is an investment project I brokered with the Rise48 sponsor team. I know the CFO and founder, and I have a direct relationship with many of the key people on the team. I have invested my own money with this group multiple times.

ACCREDITED INVESTOR: An individual or entity that meets specific income or net worth requirements as defined by securities regulations. Accredited investors are eligible to participate in certain investment opportunities that may be restricted to non-accredited investors. An accredited investor, according to the terms of the SEC, has a net worth of a million dollars and an income of $200,000 per year if single and $300,000 if married. Because the SEC may change the qualification terms in the future, the best way to know whether you are accredited is to either a) review the complete definition yourself so you can determine your status or b) talk to your CPA or wealth advisor.

The investors that came on board with that project and other projects are both **NON-ACCREDITED** and **ACCREDITED**. Being accredited means that they are higher net worth individuals earning $200,000 or $300,000 a year or more and are accredited under the terms of the Securities & Exchange Commission (SEC). A non-accredited investor, according to the terms of the SEC, has a net worth of less than a million dollars and an income of less than $200,000 per year if single and $300,000 if married.

All real estate syndication opportunities are highly regulated by the SEC. investments either fall under **REGULATION D** 506(b) or 506(c). The opportunities through Starting Point Capital are considered private placement investments, which means they are subject to specific rules. Under SEC rules, we are either allowed to advertise our investment opportunities to accredited investors (506(c)) in the public or not advertise— but only to those we have a pre-existing relationship with and who meet certain sophistication requirements (506(b)).

However, before I make these offerings available to our investors, the lead sponsor decides whether we are going to raise investor capital under the Regulation D 506(b) exemption or 506(c).

The difference is that the 506(b) allows me to raise capital from investors that have a preexisting relationship with me such as family and friends or those investors that are referred to me without a preexisting relationship. It also includes people that may have been referred to me by existing investors or people who have learned about me through LinkedIn, our podcast, or other social channels and have reached out to establish a relationship. I cannot give anyone the opportunity to invest until that relationship has existed for at least 30 days.

The downside to regulation 506(b) is that I cannot publicly advertise. I cannot put the opportunity out on LinkedIn or Instagram, and I cannot send out an email blast to people with whom I do not already have a pre-existing relationship.

NON-ACCREDITED INVESTOR: An individual or entity that does not meet the income or net worth requirements to be classified as an accredited investor. Non-accredited investors may still have access to certain investment opportunities but may have additional limitations or regulatory requirements.

REGULATION D (REG D): A provision under the U.S. federal securities law that allows companies to raise capital through the sale of equity or debt securities without having to register the offering with the SEC, providing that they meet other requirements.

But a positive is that I can accept non-accredited investors, and I can take up to 35 of them on a per-deal basis.

So far, because our opportunities historically fill up quickly, we have not found it necessary to advertise.

The relationship between the sponsor, the investors, and the fund manager ensures alignment of interest. We are all interested in a successful project, and we all have skin in the game. Compare this situation with investing in Wall Street through a financial advisor. There is limited alignment of interest there because your financial advisor makes money regardless of whether your stocks go up or down. As contrast, our investment opportunities carry a small due diligence fee, and remaining profit is not earned until after investors are made whole relative to the investments' preferred return (in most cases seven or eight percent), and it is only then that we monetize our efforts by splitting remaining profit with our investors.

Starting Point Capital is offering private investments as opposed to public investments. This means that investors can use a self-directed IRA to invest in real estate syndication opportunities, and an increasing number of people who are disenchanted by traditional investing advice are doing so.

Self-directed IRA accounts allow investors to passively invest in real estate. There is an entire industry of self-directed custodians who allow investors to tap into their IRAs and 401(k) accounts.

Here is a list of the pros and cons of using a self-directed IRA to fund passive real estate investing.

PROS OF USING A SELF-DIRECTED IRA TO FUND PASSIVE REAL ESTATE INVESTING

- A self-directed IRA is an individual retirement account for which you, the passive investor, maintain control and responsibility.
- Typical IRAs offered through your financial advisor limit your investment options to stocks, bonds, and mutual funds. With a self-directed IRA, you can invest in a wide range of investment vehicles, including real estate.
- A self-directed IRA involves the investor placing their IRA money with a custodian who is responsible only for executing the investments that the passive investor requests. The custodian does not act as a financial advisor, and they will not source or suggest specific investments— those are entirely up to you!
- With a self-directed IRA, passive investors can place their retirement capital directly into real estate opportunities.

CONS OF USING A SELF-DIRECTED IRA TO FUND PASSIVE REAL ESTATE INVESTING

- Real estate investments, like all other investments, carry risk. No asset class or investment vehicle can guarantee the passive investor a certain outcome.
- When you manage a self-directed IRA, you are fully responsible for vetting any investment you make and for learning about the tax or regulatory implications of

your investment. You cannot cast any blame upon your custodian or anyone else.
- SDIRA's must pay taxes on UBIT (Unrelated Business Income Tax) income over $1,000, which may reduce overall returns. After paying UBIT, the net returns on investments may be lower.
- When funding a passive real estate investment using a self-directed IRA, you cannot take advantage of the investment's depreciation losses.
- You also cannot take immediate possession of the passive investment's cash flow distributions or profit split (at the time of disposition) as all funds you invest using IRA money and distributions received from those investments must flow directly from and then back into your self-directed IRA.

Self-directed IRAs are one way to assign capital to passive real estate investing, and doing so is easier than you think. For more details, visit www.startingpointcapital.com/sdira.

I dive more deeply into other ways of finding capital for passive real estate investing later in Section IV.

I am often asked whether an investor should invest as an individual, with their spouse through joint ownership, or through a family trust, self-directed IRA, or an LLC. This is an important subject that is best addressed by talking to your CPA or accountant. There is no one-size-fits-all answer, and each investor's context is different.

In my case, I have invested in 29 deals as a limited partner investor, and 100 percent of them are in the name of our family trust. I have never invested in real estate syndication through an LLC because there is no liability to mitigate, which is the purpose of an LLC. I am a passive investor. The only liability I have is the unlikely event of losing my invested dollars.

THE SOFT COMMIT

When learning about a new investment opportunity, beware of the flashy pitch deck a sponsor will show you. It may be chock full of impressive numbers and aggressive timelines. People get stuck on the idea they might double their money in two to five years or see a 16 to 17 percent IRR with a 2x equity multiple. That might sound great but, in reality, you are investing in the sponsor's ability to execute the business plan, not their ability to put together a flashy investor pitch deck or presentation.

For opportunities available through Starting Point Capital, a typical business plan is acquiring and renovating a B-class apartment property. The lead sponsor will then strip the interior units down to the studs, renovate them, and increase the rents to a level that the local market can support.

From a competitive standpoint, let us say that a newly renovated two-bedroom, one-bath unit might yield $1,650 a month when complete. But that same target property today, when we acquire it, is yielding $1,200 a month. The difference in rental income, the spread or the delta, is $450. Assuming the property has 300 units and apartments sell at a multiple of net operating income, we are talking about a value creation of millions to investors. That sounds great in the pitch deck, right?

But let us be realistic for a second. Because, if there is one thing that is true in real estate, it is that things always go wrong. I like to say that birds fly, fish swim, and real estate falls apart. It is just what happens. At some point during a project, a tornado might rip through the community. There might be a serious crime like a murder on the property. These types of things happen in real life and, if you do not have the right pilot and supporting entities flying the plane, the whole thing can turn into a disaster. The team is what matters.

So, what you are really investing in are the people, the property management company, the building contractor, and the team's ability to carry out the business plan. As founder and managing partner of Starting Point Capital, I am responsible for vetting out the team that will be executing the business plan and property in which you are investing.

Here is a brief look at the benefits and drawbacks of real estate syndication so that you have some idea of what to expect.

THE BENEFITS OF REAL ESTATE SYNDICATION
- The returns often outperform Wall Street and beat inflation.
- You gain a hard asset that appreciates.
- There are significant tax benefits (see Chapter II). Seek advice from qualified tax professionals regarding the tax consequences based on your circumstances.
- Syndications provide access to larger real estate projects that are often out of reach for individual investors.
- With passive investment with professional management, the sponsors handle the property acquisition, development, and day-to-day operations.
- Investors may receive regular distributions from property income, depending upon the deal structure.

THE DRAWBACKS OF REAL ESTATE SYNDICATION
- If you choose the wrong sponsor, you could lose all of your investment.
- If you do not examine the payout structure, you could agree to invest in a financing deal that is not in your best interests.
- Limited control over investment decisions exists; the operator or general partner makes the strategic decisions.
- Illiquidity: Your capital investment will be locked into the investment until the time of a future capital event (cash out refinance or disposition).

- You must conduct due diligence and assess the track record and capabilities of the general partner or operator.
- There may be a conflict of interest if the interests of the investors and the operators are not aligned.

I have talked a lot about Starting Point Capital and its role in real estate syndication, and you are probably wondering how the company makes money.

Starting Point Capital makes money through arbitrage. For example purposes, I create the SPV whereby, depending upon the leverage of our greater investor community, the sponsor may provide Starting Point Capital's fund a 90/10 split above the preferred return. Here is how that works.

Starting Point still gets the seven to eight percent preferred return into the fund, and the sponsor splits all remaining profits. Remember, the retail investor might get a 70/30 split, but Starting Point Capital gives its investing community an 85/15 split because of the community's power to leverage.

Now, because of my service to the sponsor in finding limited partner investors, my SPV fund gets a 90/10 split. A 90/10 split versus a 70/30 (retail investor) or 85/15 split given to my investors is quite a difference when these deals go full cycle. The delta between the 90/10 that my fund is getting and the 85/15 Starting Point Capital gives to its investors is my compensation.

The next section explains the role of the different players involved in a real estate syndication deal. Let us first look at your role as a limited partner investor in the initial stages of a deal with Starting Point Capital.

As an investor and limited partner with Starting Point Capital, you will receive an email outlining an offering that we have done our own due diligence on and will be investing our own capital in. Your first job is to evaluate the offering and do your due diligence. Starting Point Capital provides an in-depth webinar that outlines the opportunity and the economic factors in the geographic locality and provides access to the UNDERWRITING and the financials.

For illustrative purposes, we will use the development of a 220-unit multifamily investment in Dallas-Fort Worth, Texas. The image below is a slide from our investor pitch deck showing the deal timeline from PURCHASE AND SALE AGREEMENT (PSA) to the monthly distributions

---

UNDERWRITING: The process of evaluating and assessing the risk to an investor of making a loan, issuing an insurance policy, or making a securities investment.

PURCHASE AND SALE AGREEMENT (PSA): This is a legal document that outlines the terms and conditions under which the buyer and seller agree to transact the sale of a property. The PSA typically covers the purchase price, closing date, contingencies, financing terms, due diligence period, and any other key terms of the deal.

DEAL TIMELINE

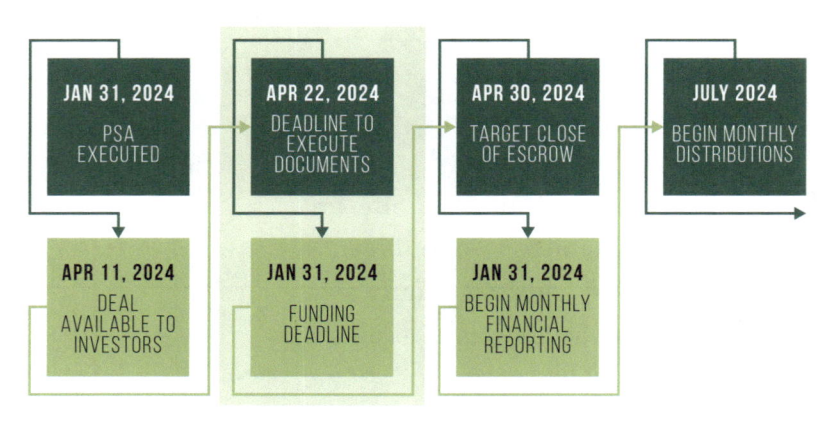

JAN 31, 2024 PSA EXECUTED	**APR 22, 2024** DEADLINE TO EXECUTE DOCUMENTS	**APR 30, 2024** TARGET CLOSE OF ESCROW	**JULY 2024** BEGIN MONTHLY DISTRIBUTIONS
APR 11, 2024 DEAL AVAILABLE TO INVESTORS	**JAN 31, 2024** FUNDING DEADLINE	**JAN 31, 2024** BEGIN MONTHLY FINANCIAL REPORTING	

The terms for the opportunity are an 85/15 split between the limited partner and the general partner (sponsor) for a $50,000 minimum investment with a seven percent preferred return.

The image below shows the investment summary for the opportunity in Dallas-Fort Worth, Texas through Starting Point Capital.

OFFERING SUMMARY

Cap Rate (T3/PF Exp)	5.05%
Projected Exit Cap Rate*	4.80%
Occupancy (03/01/2024)	91.3%
Purchase Price	$29,500,000
Equity Raise	$18,003,351
Hold Period	2-5 Years

The image below shows the rental comps for properties in the area of the opportunity in Dallas-Fort Worth, Texas through Starting Point Capital.

RENTAL COMPS

Property Name	Property Address	Year Built	Units	Distance
Fielder's Glen Apartments (Rise West Arlington)	3601 Fielders Glen Dr, Arlington, TX	1984	220	0
The Park at Ashford	3550 S Fielder Rd	1984	144	0.06
Springfield Crossing	1801 W Arkansas Ln	1984	252	1.33
Arlington Hills	3200 S Center St	1985	171	1.51
Center Place	3005 S Center St	1984	194	1.68

1 Bedrooms	Size	Rent	Rent/Sq.Ft
Arlington Hills	1,000	$1,590	$1.59
Springfield Crossing	729	$1,425	$1.95
Springfield Crossing	701	$1,400	$2.00
The Park at Ashford	801	$1,384	$1.73
Fielder's Glen	704	$1,360	$1.93
Average	725	$1,359	$1.89
Fielder's Glen	630	$1,350	$2.14
Westley Apartments	681	$1,340	$1.97
Center Place	750	$1,323	$1.76
The Park at Ashford	665	$1,235	$1.86
The Park at Ashford	585	$1,183	$2.02

2 Bedrooms	Size	Rent	Rent/Sq.Ft
Arlington Hills	1,110	$2,122	$1.91
Arlington Hills	1,068	$2,099	$1.97
The Park at Ashford	1,005	$1,906	$1.90
The Park at Ashford	1,009	$1,835	$1.82
The Park at Ashford	1,107	$1,827	$1.65
Arlington Hills	956	$1,757	$1.84
Center Place	930	$1,740	$1.87
Average	**971**	**$1,729**	**$1.78**
Fielder's Glen	966	$1,725	$1.79
Fielder's Glen	930	$1,700	$1.83
Center Place	878	$1,655	$1.88
Arlington Hills	936	$1,654	$1.77
Springfield Crossing	888	$1,625	$1.83
Springfield Crossing	878	$1,575	$1.79
Arlington Hills	916	$1,510	$1.65
The Park at Ashford	993	$1,200	$1.21

There are no direct comps for the studio bedroom apartments located at Fielder's Glen. Costar only had two properties: Lenox Cooper (2023 build) and Ten Twelve West (1969 build). Therefore, we did not include the comps here as we determined that the two properties were not appropriate comps for Fielder's Glen. The studio bedroom units are over $250+ cheaper than our renovated 1 bedroom apartments and we feel confident in being able to achieve these rents without any issues.

Looking at the rental comps within a five or ten-mile radius is one way to stress test the business plan, but there are lots of others.

Look at the capital expenditures and the underwriting process. Let us say that the business plan is to spend $16,000 per unit, and the project is targeting a 250-unit property and renovating all 250 of the classic units. If the underwriting process determines that, to actually produce a 16 percent annual internal rate of return (IRR), the rents will have to be raised by $200—but the local market comparables show that there is only room for a $75 a month in rent growth—there is no point moving forward.

Common resources to research comps are RealPage and CoStar. The expected exit cap rate is also critical. The NET OPERATING INCOME (NOI) and the eventual EXIT CAP RATE are assessed on a multiplier and used to calculate the exit price.

Nobody knows what the actual exit cap rate will be for the target investment in five years from now because there are too many unknown variables. One of those unknown variables is deferred maintenance. Let us say a property was built in the 1980s and has a laundry list of tenant requests for maintenance. For example, the ceiling is leaking in one unit, a washer and dryer are not working in another, and there is a

NET OPERATING INCOME (NOI): A calculation used to analyze real estate investments that generate income. NOI equals all revenue from the property minus all reasonably necessary operating expenses.

EXIT CAP RATE: An estimate of a property's potential resale value at the end of its holding period.

massive crack in the sidewalk. All these issues could indicate that the sponsor is struggling with maintaining occupancy and cannot push rents.

If these issues, known as deferred maintenance, are apparent, it might be a good idea to check if the business plan includes a strategy to decrease the deferred maintenance. The renovations budget should address future deferred maintenance issues.

One way that a sponsor can drastically manipulate the IRR and the equity multiple is by adjusting what the projected exit cap rate is. If you decrease the projected exit cap rate by 25 basis points, it is compressed, which increases the exit valuations. You could be talking about an IRR projection that is 200 basis points higher or an equity multiple that is 30 or 40 basis points higher just by manipulating what you project the exit cap rate is going to be in the future.

Starting Point Capital prefers to partner with operators and sponsors that provide an exit cap spread or range. For example, if the exit cap rate is 4.5 percent, then your IRR projection would look like X. If the exit cap rate is expanded to 5.5 percent, then your IRR and equity multiple would look like Y. This is preferable to fleshing out an overly optimistic exit cap rate when nobody has a crystal ball.

There are many terms to look out for when reviewing the underwriting, and I will go into the more technical terms in the next section. However, one important term to look for is LOSS TO LEASE.

Let us say Property A was built in the 1980s or 1990s, and all the units are outdated. The owner might get a rent of $1,200 a month for a two-bedroom, one-bath unit. However, a competitor property across the street, Property B, has already been fully renovated. Both properties have equal amenities and are in a B-class neighborhood, but Property B is getting $1,600 for a similarly sized two-bedroom, one-bath unit.

> **LOSS TO LEASE:** One of the most essential metrics in multifamily real estate, it can be defined as the difference between actual rent and market rent. In general, this income is lost by offering incentives to encourage tenants to sign or renew their lease.

The delta between the $1,200 from property A and the $1,600 is $400. That is what is called loss to lease. Another way to explain it is that the sponsor who is buying the target property, who knows that the competitive asset across the street is going to be able to achieve a $400 rent premium or increase, is burning off loss to lease or the value that they know they can get in the market. The term loss to lease would appear in the financial projections for cash flow.

Basically, loss to lease is an underwriting term that the investor can use to stress-test the financials. They can look at the current rents versus the comp rents within a five-mile radius of the potential target investment, which will tell the investor whether the sponsor is being overly aggressive or conservative in their estimations of future rents.

There are many more aspects to understanding and assessing a syndication deal, and I will delve into what to look for in the next section.

As the investor, if you are satisfied with and hopefully excited by the opportunity, then the next step is the soft commit. This is where you reserve a spot in the opportunity, so to speak. The soft commit indicates how much you are interested in investing in that specific opportunity. The minimum is typically $50,000, and many of our investors want to invest more than that and will invest in multiple opportunities.

PRIVATE PLACEMENT MEMORANDUM (PPM): The PPM provides detailed information about the investment opportunity, including the terms, risks, and other pertinent disclosures that potential investors need to consider before making an investment decision. It serves as a comprehensive offering document that outlines the investment opportunity and helps potential investors to make informed choices.

The opportunities fill up quickly—with Rise Sun Valley that I introduced at the beginning of the book being an example. That opportunity filled up within hours. It is not uncommon for me to send an email outlining an opportunity at 8:30 a.m. and for that opportunity to be fully subscribed by 2 p.m. on that same day.

Once the investors are accepted, the limited partner will review and sign the subscription documents, also known as the operating documents or the PRIVATE PLACEMENT MEMORANDUM (PPM).

These are a set of legal documents provided by the general partner detailing the investment terms, the company's financials, the risks involved, and the underwriting.

If the limited partner is satisfied with the investment summary, the final step in the investing process is the hard commit, which is to wire funds to the investment by the funding deadline. Then, the excitement begins!

IV
FRAMING OUT

If you are still turning the pages in this book, you are likely intrigued by new ways of investing and may already have dabbled in other money-making activities like day trading or fixing and flipping. If that is the case, then you will know the two golden rules when it comes to investing:
1. Never invest money you cannot afford to lose.
2. Always conduct thorough due diligence and carefully vet both the investment and the individuals involved.

This chapter will explain how to do your due diligence for a real estate syndication investment.

I emphasize throughout this book how the success of a real estate syndication investment depends almost exclusively upon the sponsor, or the operator, of the project. So, vetting the sponsor is the most critical component of doing your due diligence for passive real estate investing. It is as important as vetting a startup for a SEED CAPITAL investment.

SEED CAPITAL: Capital raised to begin developing an idea for a business or a new product.

I have extensive experience in investing as an angel investor through seed rounds. Seed rounds are the earliest rounds of startup investing, and friends and family usually fund these rounds. Some of that experience stems from my role as a member of Gopher Angels, a Minnesota-based investment community launched in 2012 by lifelong entrepreneurs David and Sara Russick. Gopher Angels was an outgrowth of the Carlson School of Management at the University of Minnesota. The group is Minnesota's largest and most active angel investor network. Its members invest in high-potential startups and provide a value-add experience for entrepreneurs from all industries.

Every quarter, the group brings in entrepreneurs to pitch their ideas and to explain why we should invest in their company at the seed round. The event is a lot like the popular TV show, *Shark Tank*, where the entrepreneur gives a 40-minute, nerve-wracking pitch to a panel of celebrity investors. But the most interesting aspect of the show is that the entrepreneurs are grilled by the panel, and any holes in their business plan or financials are quickly exposed. Obviously, the investors do not want to invest in an idea that will not make money.

Angel investing is highly risky, and the truth is that any money given to entrepreneurs and startups at the early stages typically becomes a donation. That said, the one out of

10 times that a product or idea is a success, that investment can go to the moon. You could invest $50,000 into something, and it turns into two and a half million. More often than not, though, you are losing your $50,000.

In my capacity as a fund manager with Starting Point Capital, I take the time to grill any sponsor with whom I intend to work. I liken it to the dating process. I will find out as much as I can about their deals and operations for a long time before I decide to work with them and recommend them to my network of investors. I am "dating" a few at the moment. I have married several best-in-class sponsors and do not intend to divorce them, but I will also consider entering into long-term business relationships with other sponsors once I have invested with them myself and seen the results.

The two golden rules that apply to any investing strategy apply to passive real estate syndication. How much you can afford to lose is up to you and your budgeting prowess. Due diligence needs to be thorough and focused upon the sponsors of any deal you are considering, the business plan, and the deal structure.

Of course, the biggest risk is unscrupulous or incompetent sponsors. If you take away nothing else from this book, take away the importance of choosing the right sponsor or general partner. Another risk is agreeing to a deal structure that is not in your best interests.

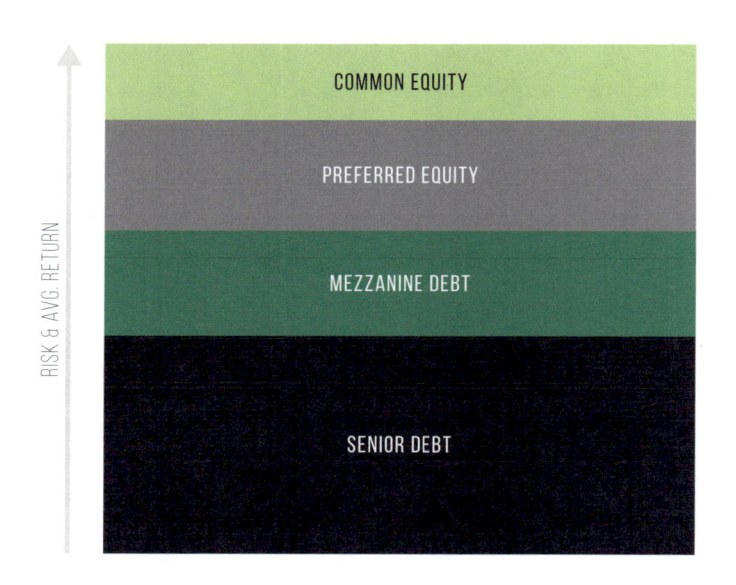

THE CAPITAL STACK

[Diagram: A stacked bar chart with a vertical axis labeled "RISK & AVG. RETURN" pointing upward. From bottom to top: SENIOR DEBT (black), MEZZANINE DEBT (green), PREFERRED EQUITY (gray), COMMON EQUITY (light green).]

To understand the deal structure of real estate syndication, you should be familiar with the capital stack. The capital stack is the overall structure for the project. If you invest in a real estate project, the capital stack will dictate how much risk you are exposed to and how and when you will be paid.

There are four layers to the real estate capital stack: **Common equity, preferred equity, mezzanine debt**, and **senior debt**. Some capital stack structures have fewer layers, such as just debt and equity, and others have more.

At the base of the stack is senior debt. Senior debt is paid out first, followed by the mezzanine debt, preferred equity and, finally, common equity. If the real estate investment does not perform as projected, there may not be enough money to repay all funds invested along with returns. In this case, the senior lender (the base of the capital stack) is paid first and other layers in the stack thereafter.

The projected return generally corresponds to the amount of risk. While investing in the bottom of the capital stack is typically more secure, it also generates lower returns. Conversely, investing at the top of the capital stack is less secure, but there tends to be more upside potential.

Common equity is the top layer of the capital stack. It is the riskiest layer because it is the last to get paid. This is the layer of the capital stack where limited partners invest. However, it is potentially the most rewarding due to its higher returns. Common equity often does not have a recorded secured interest in the property, nor is it typically entitled to recurring payments, so you may not see any return until the property is sold. If the investment does not perform as projected, you are potentially at risk of losing some or all of your initial investment.

The upside is that potential returns typically are not capped for common equity investors. Thus, in the event that the investment is largely successful, common equity investors could realize very sizable returns.

The project sponsors often co-invest at this level, too, which gives them incentive to maximize the returns for everyone in the stack. They want a return, too, and they will only receive profit participation if everyone else does.

Preferred equity sits just below the common equity layer. Investors here typically receive a preferred rate of return that must be paid before the common equity layer, so it is less risky. Mezzanine debt is a type of financing that sits between senior debt (secured by the property) and equity in the capital stack. It is typically used in the initial financing of a real estate project or during a recapitalization. It functions as a hybrid of debt and equity, providing the lender with the right to convert to an equity interest in the event of default. The preferred equity layer will typically share in some (though less) of the upside of the investment and may have a right to regular recurring payments.

Payment for mezzanine-level investors comes after any senior debt investors and before the equity layers. Mezzanine debt investors will typically receive regular payments at a stated rate not tied to the performance of the investment, and that rate may be higher than the senior debt rate because of the increased risk. Like equity, mezzanine debt investors will typically have a right to share in a portion of the potential profits but a much lower portion than the equity layers.

Mezzanine debt is not typically secured by a recorded interest in the property itself. The mezzanine debt layer means you share in some of the potential upside while also securing a guaranteed right to payment at a lower position in the capital stack. Also, mezzanine debt investors may have limited foreclosure rights.

Senior debt is the largest, least risky, and least expensive portion of the capital stack. Capital at this level usually comes from a bank and is secured by a deed of trust or a mortgage recorded against the property. Investors at this level benefit from regular interest payments at a stated rate not tied to the ultimate performance or success of the investment.

Because of its lower relative risk, returns for senior debt investments are also lower. Investors are paid first but do not share in any of the potential upside or profits of the venture.

That explains the capital stack, which gives you a picture of where you stand when it comes to payouts and risk. Let us take a closer look at the interest rates on the debt.

There are two common types of loans or debt—FIXED-RATE DEBT and FLOATING-RATE DEBT. A fixed-rate loan is traditionally obtained through Fannie Mae or Freddie Mac, the two large institutional real estate lenders, or through a community bank. A floating-rate loan is often referred to as bridge debt.

FIXED-RATE DEBT: A loan that has a fixed interest rate for the entire term of the loan, providing predictable monthly payments.

FLOATING-RATE DEBT: A loan whereby banks and financial institutions charge a spread over the benchmark rate based upon factors such as the type of asset and the consumer's credit rating. A floating rate might be the LIBOR plus 300 basis points.

JEREMY DYER

FLOATING-RATE BRIDGE VS. FIXED-RATE LOANS

When evaluating financing options for real estate investments, understanding the differences between floating-rate bridge loans and long-term, fixed-rate debt structures is crucial. Each has its place, depending upon your strategy and market conditions.

Floating-rate bridge loans are typically short-term, used to finance properties that may need renovation or repositioning before stabilization. The interest rate on a floating-rate loan fluctuates with the market, but a going-in purchased rate cap can limit how high the rate can go, providing some level of protection against extreme rate hikes. This flexibility can be advantageous in a rising interest rate environment, like the one we have experienced recently, allowing investors to exit or refinance when the property is stabilized and the value is higher.

However, there is a trade-off. While floating-rate bridge loans offer flexibility, they can also come with higher short-term costs, including the cost of purchasing the rate cap itself. Investors must be confident in their ability to execute their business plan within the loan's term to avoid potential refinancing risks.

On the other hand, long-term, fixed-rate debt provides stability and predictability. These loans lock in an interest rate for the duration of the term, which can be beneficial in a low or stable interest rate environment. Investors who plan to hold a property for a longer term may prefer this option to avoid the volatility associated with floating rates. It is a conservative approach that protects against rate hikes and ensures consistent debt service payments.

The downside? Fixed-rate loans often come with PREPAYMENT PENALTIES or yield maintenance, making it costly to exit the loan early if market conditions change or a more favorable refinancing option becomes available. This can limit flexibility if the business plan calls for the renovations to be completed in 18-24 months, stabilized and, depending upon local market conditions, ready to be sold.

> **PREPAYMENT PENALTY:** A fee that lenders might charge if a loan is paid off before the end of its term. It compensates the lender for the interest payments they lose due to early repayment.

Which is better? There is no one-size-fits-all answer. The choice between these debt structures depends upon your investment strategy, risk tolerance, and market outlook. Floating-rate bridge loans with a rate cap might be suitable for opportunistic investments that require agility while long-term, fixed-rate debt is often favored for stable, cash-flowing assets with a long-term hold strategy.

In the end, the key is aligning your financing structure with your investment goals and market expectations. Understanding the trade-offs will help you to make informed decisions and optimize your returns.

For a thorough look into structuring debt for multifamily real estate, there is no better resource than a book written by Rob Beardsley, *Structuring and Raising Debt & Equity for Real Estate*.

The image below shows the debt financing for the Rise West Arlington opportunity in Dallas-Fort Worth, Texas previously offered through Starting Point Capital. This opportunity had a floating interest rate on the debt but with a cap at 4.75 percent.

DEBT FINANCING

Initial Loan Amount	$18,570,918	(63% of purchase price/63% LTV)
Future Funding	$5,929,082	(100% of CapEx Funding)
Interest Rate Cap (Maximum)	4.75%	
Interest only period	Full Term	
Term	3+1+1 (5 years)	
Fixed or Floating	Floating with Interest Rate Cap – 4.75%	
Prepayment Penalty	No Prepayment Penalty	

We are buying the interest rate down by purchasing an interest rate cap that caps our total interest at 4.75%. Our maximum interest rate is 4.75% and it cannot exceed this. The returns we are projecting are assuming the maximum interest rate of 4.75%. If the Fed continues to increase the interest rates, it will not impact your returns or the underwriting for this investment.

People often assume that fixed-rate debt is better for a real estate syndication deal because, if interest rates go up, there is no effect. For loans with a five-year term or more, that might be the best option. But what if the business plan is to renovate all the units and sell the property in two to five years?

If an operator has a fixed-rate loan of five years and decides to sell in two years, the bank is going to assess the owner of the property for YIELD MAINTENANCE or defeasance and charge the delta of the interest that it would have received over the course of the next three years. So, in this case, the fixed-rate loan is not the best strategy, and a bridge loan may be the preferred one.

A fixed-rate loan would fit a business plan where the goal is to build a brand-new apartment building from the ground up such as a BUILD-TO-RENT (BTR) project.

It will take two years to build a property and a year to lease it out. If the strategy is to hold the

YIELD MAINTENANCE: Yield maintenance dictates that borrowers pay the rate differential between the loan interest rate and the prevailing market interest rate on the prepaid capital for the period remaining to loan maturity.

BUILD TO RENT (BTR): Constructing residential properties with the primary purpose of renting them out to tenants. Unlike traditional real estate development where properties are built for sale, BTR properties are designed to create a consistent stream of rental income.

> **DEBT SERVICE:** The total amount of money required to cover the repayment of interest and principal on a debt for a specific time period. It is a key figure in determining the cash flow and profitability of an investment.

> **DEBT SERVICE COVERAGE RATIO (DSCR):** A measure of the cash flow available to pay current debt obligations, calculated by dividing the net operating income by the total debt service. A DSCR of less than one indicates a negative cash flow.

property and pay investors an eight or nine percent return without much equity upside on the backend but leveraging the cash flow, in this scenario, a fixed-rate loan is the better option.

Inflation plays a huge role in real estate syndication financing. The Federal Reserve will typically increase interest rates to tackle inflation. Interest rates skyrocketed in late 2021 and early 2022, which took everyone by surprise. Best-in-class sponsors purchase rate caps to de-risk projects for investors, which means that the interest rate on their loans cannot go above a certain level for a defined period, typically three years and those sponsors secured lower leverage loans and raised sufficient equity on the front end to extend the loan.

Just prior to late 2020 and 2021, the general consensus had been that interest rates would remain low or go up 200 basis points at most. To tackle inflation, the federal funds rate actually went up 550 basis points. Unfortunately, some sponsors had acquired floating-rate bridge loans without purchasing a rate cap—rate caps are expensive. These sponsors were caught with their pants down as the tide went out. They could not afford the debt because interest rates increased from 3.5 percent to, in some cases, over nine percent almost overnight. Suddenly, their DEBT SERVICE COVERAGE RATIO (DSCR) was below one, and they were no longer cash-flowing at the property level.

Rise48, for example, one of the sponsors that Starting Point Capital partners with, acquires an interest rate cap to cap the total interest rate (inclusive of the lender spread and the index) at 4.75 percent to protect their investors in the event that interest rates remain at historically elevated levels or continue upward. Even if rates rise, the loans are still at the strike price or going-in rate cap of 4.75 percent. Consequently, if rates decline below the in-place rate cap, that will benefit the overall investment.

An investment summary might reference the RETURN OF CAPITAL. That is not the same as RETURN ON CAPITAL.

RETURN OF CAPITAL: A distribution to investors from the sponsor that is not based upon profit but a markup added at the initial investment stage. It can be designed to manage investor expectations.]

RETURN ON CAPITAL: A distribution to investors that is based on real income at the property level.

A return of capital occurs when an investor invests $100,000 and starts to receive distributions that are not tied directly to any real business plan improvements. The investor might be receiving a distribution every month, but the sponsor is actually just giving them a deposit back generated from surplus capital they purposefully over-raised.

Let us say a sponsor is raising $18 million. They may only need to raise $16 million from investors but, instead, raise $18 million so that they can pay distributions immediately to keep investors happy. Call it managing expectations.

On the other hand, return on capital is when the investment is actually producing a distribution to the investor based upon real income or operating income at the property level. You, the investor, are receiving that distribution based upon real revenues and real profits.

This is one area where you would be wise to challenge the sponsor and ask them how much of the capital they are raising is set aside for a rainy day fund for emergency purposes. Ask them whether, on day one, are they just giving some of that back to investors as a return *of* capital or is it a return *on* their capital?

So far, I have painted a rosy picture of passive real estate investing, but I have also made clear that there is a risk that you could lose some, or all, of your investment. However, that is where risk mitigation comes down to finding the right sponsor.

A CAPITAL CALL occurs because the bank is requiring the sponsor team to put more money into the deal to buy down the debt, usually because the debt payment has increased, or the sponsor does not have enough operating income to support the debt service.

Let us say that a sponsor acquired a property in 2021, and the monthly debt service payment is $100,000. Now, the interest rate on the mortgage has doubled because the sponsor did not purchase a rate cap. The debt payment is now $150,000 to $175,000 per month.

Cash flow is strained, and the debt service coverage ratio goes to one or below one. If the sponsor does not pump more LIQUIDITY into the deal, they run the risk of foreclosure on the asset or the bank might force them to sell at a loss.

Sponsors in this type of situation might be forced to ask their investors for additional capital to maintain liquidity at the property level, perhaps putting in an additional 30 percent to the deal. Thus, an investor who initially put in $100,000 now has to put in another $30,000. The investor could choose not to participate but, potentially, their shares could be diluted.

> **CAPITAL CALL:** A request made by a syndication or fund for a portion of the money promised by an investor, used to fund operations or investment purchases. It is a call for the investor to fulfill their commitment.

> **LIQUIDITY:** The ability to quickly convert an asset into cash without significantly impacting its price. Real estate is typically considered a less liquid asset.

If enough limited partner investors choose not to participate, everybody runs the risk of losing up to 100 percent of their investment because the bank may foreclose upon the asset.

Capital calls do happen, particularly if you do not select the right sponsor. Starting Point Capital, however, has never raised capital on an opportunity with a sponsor that has initiated a capital call.

It is also important to understand that a sponsor might stage a capital call—not because they are doing an ineffective job at asset management or operations but because their debt service spiked, and it was not in the business plan for their interest rate to go from 3.5 to 7.5 percent or more. The distress is financial and not operational in many cases.

Many best-in-class sponsors have experienced capital calls in recent years. Perhaps they gambled and did not purchase a rate cap on a bridge loan. What counts is what they are doing now in response to the event. I have experienced my own capital calls on some of my own deals, but this has been instrumental in my education in vetting out best-in-class operators.

What that operator does to minimize the impact of a capital call on the limited partner investors is indicative of whether they are best in class. Some operators are willing to give up a percentage of their own acquisition fees, asset under management fees, profit participation split, and so forth in exchange for your participation in a capital call.

Other best-in-class operators will provide a low interest to a no-interest loan for the property. For example, if the bank requires a sponsor to raise $2 million through a capital call from their limited partner investor base, the sponsor might offer to provide a no-interest loan to cover a million of that $2 million. Now, they require only half to be contributed by the limited partners.

The sponsor might also give up all their asset management fee. Many sponsors charge an asset management fee of one to three percent per year. If they are navigating a capital call, that fee will keep the lights on. Remember, the sponsor's compensation on these deals is limited until they go full cycle, so they need to charge an asset management fee to pay for the in-house staff, the lease on office space, and whatever the overheads are. Some sponsors will decrease or cease charging the asset management fee in a gesture of good faith.

If the sponsor reacts in this way, an investor is more likely to reinvest with them in the future. That sponsor has shown a willingness to put their limited partner investors ahead of their own interests. They may even be willing to forgo a percentage of their general partner equity profit split, known as the PROMOTE, that they receive at the end when that deal goes full cycle.

PROMOTE: Also known as the equity profit split, the promote is how the profits from an opportunity are to be distributed among the limited partners and the general partner (sponsor). For example, in an 85/15 split, the limited partners will get 85 percent of the profits, and the general partner will receive 15 percent.

By maintaining a healthy and transparent relationship with their investors, sponsors can be confident that those investors will be on board when they target another deal six months from now.

WHY THE SPONSOR IS CONCERN NUMBER ONE

Capital calls aside, because they are a rarity, the sponsor is the most important factor in any real estate project. They are the pilot of the plane.

Choosing the right sponsor is the key to success in real estate syndication because, not only will the right sponsor manage a project well, but they will choose the right deals that align best for the investor. It is just that simple. I will go into how to find the right sponsors and deals in detail a bit later.

So, the investor needs to do some due diligence and ask some key questions. Has the sponsor done this before? Has the sponsor experienced adversity and come out on the other side? For example, how did they weather the global financial crisis? How did they fare when the Federal Reserve aggressively increased the SOFR rate from virtually zero to 5.5 percent?

Debt costs have skyrocketed, and many sponsors had floating-rate loans because, in 2021, they assumed that borrowing costs would sit at 3.5 percent forever. Instead, they practically doubled overnight. How did the sponsors fend off that curve ball?

What does the business plan look like? Has the sponsor stress-tested the financials under various scenarios? For example, what if the occupancy rate in a multifamily property goes from 95 percent to 60 percent because somebody decided to build a brand-new apartment building across the street, and everybody decided to relocate there? Have they stress-tested a scenario where a major employer decides to leave that market? For example, in 2008 and 2009, all the automotive plants in Detroit, Michigan virtually shut down, wrecking the local economy.

If the investor does all their due diligence, and the project still looks good, it should be a go. At that point, my role with Starting Point Capital is to represent the sponsor to the investors as a reliable sponsor that ticks all the boxes.

Here is the good news to keep in mind when considering a syndication deal: When the investing group acquires assets, even with no renovations to a multifamily building, that building will still produce cash flow. For any investment that Starting Point Capital is involved in, the sponsors, investors, and I must have confidence that that investment will produce anywhere between a four to seven percent average cash-on-cash returns even if nobody ever swings a hammer or makes any improvements to the interior or exterior of the property.

JEREMY DYER

SINGLE VS. MULTIFAMILY VALUATIONS

When it comes to real estate investing, understanding how properties are valued is important. The approach to valuing single-family homes is quite different from how multifamily properties are priced. These differences are essential for investors to grasp, especially if you are considering expanding your portfolio from residential to multifamily assets.

The value of a single-family home is primarily determined by market comparables or "comps." This means that the price of a home is based upon what similar homes in the same area have recently sold for. Factors like square footage, number of bedrooms and bathrooms, lot size, and the condition of the property all play a role. However, single-family home values are also influenced by more subjective factors such as curb appeal, neighborhood desirability, school districts, and even the overall market sentiment.

In the single-family market, buyers often have an emotional connection to the property—they are purchasing a place to live, not just an investment. This emotional aspect can drive prices up, especially in competitive markets where buyers might be willing to pay more than the calculated market value to secure their ideal home.

In contrast, multifamily properties are valued based upon their income-generating potential. The primary metric used to determine the value of a multifamily property is its net operating income (NOI)—the total income generated from the property minus operating expenses (excluding mortgage payments).

Multifamily properties are typically priced on a multiple of their NOI, known as the capitalization rate or "cap rate." The cap rate represents the expected rate of return on the property and varies, depending upon the market, property type, and perceived risk. The value of the property is essentially the NOI divided by the cap rate.

For example, if a value-add multifamily business plan increased the NOI by $100,000 and the market cap rate is five percent, the sponsor would have effectively increased the exit value of the property by $2 million ($100,000 ÷ 0.05 = $2,000,000). This method of valuation is more objective and rooted in the financial performance of the property rather than comparable sales or emotional appeal.

By trading at a multiple of NOI, multifamily properties offer investors a clearer understanding of the potential return on their investment, making them an attractive option for those looking to build a robust real estate portfolio.

PRICE PER DOOR

When underwriting multifamily real estate, price per door is a key metric that investors use to evaluate and compare properties. It is a quick way to assess the cost of each unit within a property, helping investors to determine whether they are getting a good deal relative to other properties in the same market. However, while price per door is valuable, it is essential to understand its limitations—especially when comparing properties across different tertiary markets.

The price per door provides a baseline for understanding the cost structure of a multifamily property. It allows investors to quickly gauge whether a property is priced in line with others in the area and helps to identify opportunities where the cost per unit might be lower than average, potentially signaling a value-add opportunity.

One of the often-overlooked factors when considering price per door is the property's unit mix—the distribution of different types of units within the property such as studios, one-bedrooms, two-bedrooms, and so on. The value and demand for these units can vary significantly, depending upon the local market dynamics. For example, a property with a high percentage of larger, family-oriented units may command a different price per door than one dominated by smaller, single-occupancy units even within the same market.

Moreover, the local competitive market for these specific unit types plays a crucial role. A property might have a low price per door but, if the local market is saturated with similar units or if the demand for the specific unit mix is low, this could impact the property's ability to maintain high occupancy rates and justify the investment.

When you start comparing price per door across different tertiary markets, things get even more complex. Markets vary widely in terms of economic conditions, population trends, rental demand, corporate employers in the area, and competitive landscapes. A property with a seemingly low price per door in one market may not be as advantageous as a higher-priced property in another market with stronger demand, better economic prospects, or a more favorable unit mix.

Additionally, cap rates, which reflect the perceived risk and return of a property, differ across markets. A low price per door in a high-cap-rate market might signal higher risk or lower demand while a higher price per door in a low-cap-rate market might indicate a premium property in a stable, high-demand area.

In real estate, context is everything. Use price per door as a starting point, but always pair it with a thorough analysis of the property's unit mix, local competition, and market conditions to ensure you are making a well-informed investment decision.

MARKET ABSORPTION RATE

Understanding the economic impact of absorption rates in multifamily real estate is crucial for any investor looking to de-risk their deals. Absorption rates measure the pace at which newly delivered units are leased in a given market. These rates provide valuable insights into the supply and demand dynamics that can make or break an investment.

When new multifamily developments come online, the absorption rate indicates how quickly tenants are occupying these units. A high absorption rate suggests strong demand, signaling that the market can comfortably handle the new supply without significant pressure on rental rates or occupancy levels. On the other hand, a low absorption rate may indicate an oversupply of units, leading to increased vacancy rates, downward pressure on rents and, ultimately, a weaker financial performance for investors.

Starting Point Capital primarily focuses on good neighborhoods, acquiring the property at a good basis and forcing appreciation through a value-add business plan.

That means that, even if organic appreciation goes in the negative in the local market (perhaps the occupancy wanes and we cannot hit our PRO FORMA projections in terms of rental income), we stay resolute on forcing

---

PRO FORMA:
A set of financial projections for a real estate investment, which estimates the expected returns, operating expenses, and cash flow.

VACANCY RATE:
The percentage of all available units in a rental property, such as an apartment complex or office building, that are vacant or unoccupied at a particular time.

that appreciation through a value-add business plan.

Let us say a target property is 97 percent occupied. How are we going to renovate 300 of these units if we have 97 percent occupancy? We have to intentionally force VACANCY. We need to free up units to renovate, which we do by either non-renewing the tenant's lease or by offering incentives to tenants.

Forced vacancy is intentionally driving down occupancy from, say, 97 percent to 92 percent. The incentives offered to tenants might be for them to temporarily move to a fully renovated unit across the hallway in return for some CONCESSIONS— perhaps a month or two with no rent due.

During peak leasing season, typically in the spring and summer, a sponsor might provide some incentives for new residents to move in. These are called concessions, and they are important because they add up to lost revenue. It is important that sponsors ensure they are providing concessions, when appropriate, but are balancing them with burning off those concessions.

CONCESSION:
A discount or incentive offered to a tenant, often used to entice them to sign a lease. Examples include reduced rent for a certain period or a landlord making improvements to the leased space at their own expense.

LEASEHOLD IMPROVEMENT:
Alterations made to rental premises to customize it for the specific needs of a tenant. These improvements will typically revert to the landlord upon termination of the lease.

There is a difference between physical occupancy and economic occupancy. Physical occupancy is how many bodies are living in the units. Ninety-seven percent occupancy is physical occupancy, but that is not economic occupancy. Just because 97 percent of units are occupied does not mean that a sponsor is collecting rents based upon 97 percent occupancy. Why? Because there may be some concessions.

Here is an example of how we force appreciation and what the material impact is when the investors exit the project.

Let us look at a recent deal I launched as an illustrative example. This deal is a multifamily development project where the business plan includes putting washers and dryers in every unit. The building was built in 1984. It has 353 units, and none of them have a washer and dryer. The plan is to install washers and dryers in every unit because we know that the competitive assets in that area, Fort Worth, Texas, have washers and dryers in the units. We can charge the tenants an additional $50 per month just by putting in a washer and dryer in their unit. The tenants usually like this idea and are not resistant to the upgrades.

Now, if you spread $50 per month over 353 units at a conservative capitalization (cap) rate, that is the relationship between the return on income and what we expect the asset to sell for in the future. The returns calculation uses a GOING-IN CAP RATE and an EXIT CAP RATE.

The going-in cap rate is the net operating income divided by the purchase price. The exit cap rate is the future net operating income that we forced that is now divided by the exit valuation or price. So, at a conservative 4.8 percent cap rate, $50 per unit just for washer and dryers at a 4.8 percent exit cap rate equals $4 million.

That is the increase in the property's valuation before we ever think about renovating a kitchen or bathroom or putting in a new swimming pool.

That $4 million is split 85 percent to the limited partners and 15 percent to the sponsor. The share that the limited partner investors receive depends upon their share of the ownership. For example, if a project raises $10 million, and an investor has put in $100,000, their $100,000 is one percent of $10 million. Therefore, the investor would receive one percent of the 85 percent of the $4 million, which is $34,000 of unrealized investor equity just for putting in washers and dryers.

GOING-IN CAP RATE: The going-in cap rate is the projected first-year net of income (NOI) divided by the initial investment or purchase price.

EXIT CAP RATE: The capitalization rate used to estimate the sell price of a property at the end of the holding period. It helps investors estimate their potential return when planning to exit the investment.

The amount that the investor receives when the property is sold is called equity profit split or the promote. Cash-on-cash refers to the distributions that the investor receives over the course of the hold period. At Starting Point Capital, we typically pay distributions monthly or quarterly, depending upon the deal. Then, there is the preferred rate of return, which is cumulative. So, if the preferred annual rate of return is seven or eight percent, we are going to make that investor whole at that preferred rate of return when we exit the deal. When we sell the property, even though the average annual cash on cash might be 5.5 percent, our preferred return is seven percent over a three-to-five-year hold, which means we need to get the investors caught up.

Once we get them caught up to the preferred return, then all remaining profits that are left over are split between the sponsor and the limited partners.

DISTRESSED SELLERS AND SPONSORS

Let us talk about distressed sellers and sponsors for a minute because not all sponsors in the business of acquiring, managing, and disposing of commercial real estate are equal. A distressed seller or sponsor could be somebody who currently owns the targeted property we want to invest in but is distressed on the operations side of the business.

Let us say the Federal Reserve increases the SOFR from basically zero percent to 5.5 percent over a 16-month period. As the rate increases, the sponsor must pay the bank a higher amount to cover their debt payments. That has a drastic effect upon the cash flow the sponsor receives from the property, potentially to the extent that the revenues are less than the expenses.

Because the senior lender is the largest single investor, the bank is monitoring the financials on a monthly basis as well as the cash flow. The bank also takes note of the debt service coverage ratio (DSCR), which is a measure of the cash flow available to pay current debt obligations. A DSCR of less than one indicates negative cash flow and that revenues and expenses are equal. A healthy DSCR is at least 1.25x or higher.

A DSCR that falls below 1.00x indicates a property bleeding cash. At that point, the bank is likely to call the sponsor and suggest a capital call to pump in some more liquidity into the asset. Another option is for the sponsor to sell the property at a loss. Sometimes, an opportunistic sponsor will acquire a financially distressed property if the DSCR is below one.

The image below shows the five-year pro-forma projections along with the DSCR for the Rise West Arlington opportunity in Dallas-Fort Worth, Texas through Starting Point Capital.

* *represents total taxes escrowed during the year. Refer to "Tax Projections" slide for additional information on tax forecasts.*

5 YEAR PRO-FORMA

Rental Income	T12	T3	T3
Gross potential rent	$3,325,743	$3,325,743	$3,325,743
Less: Economic vacancy	604,458	399,204	399,204
% Economic Vacancy	18.2%	12.0%	12.0%
Total rent revenue	$2,721,285	$2,926,539	$2,926,539
YoY change			
Other income	495,313	495,313	495,313
Total operating income	$3,216,597	$3,421,852	$3,421,852
Operating Expenses	T12	T12	PF Exp
R&M, Turnover, and CS	177,178	177,178	198,791
Payroll	289,454	289,454	308,000
Admin & Marketing	118,574	118,574	121,042
Property Management Fee	96,504	96,504	102,656
Property taxes*	724,818	724,818	592,037
Insurance	238,710	238,710	217,800
Utilities	256,840	256,840	264,545
Replacement reserves	55,000	55,000	55,000
Total Expenses	1,957,077	1,957,077	1,859,871
Net Operating Income	$1,259,520	$1,464,774	$1,561,981
YoY change			
Debt Service			
DSCR			
Equity Management Fees			
Free cash flow			
Operational reserve release			
Net Proceeds (On sale or Refi)			
Total distributable cash flow			

	Year 1	Year 2	Year 3	Year 4	Year 5
	$3,358,896	$3,659,041	$4,049,937	$4,257,527	$4,387,024
	546,785	487,010	444,885	340,602	350,962
	16.3%	13.3%	11.0%	8.0%	8.0%
	$2,812,111	**$3,172,031**	**$3,605,052**	**$3,916,925**	**$4,036,062**
	3.3%	12.8%	13.7%	8.7%	3.0%
	523,966	602,311	672,755	758,251	772,282
	$3,336,076	**$3,774,342**	**$4,277,807**	**$4,675,176**	**$4,808,344**

$/unit/yr.	Year 1	Year 2	Year 3	Year 4	Year 5
1,232	271,013	275,081	279,272	289,141	296,283
1,400	308,000	317,240	326,757	336,560	346,657
550	121,042	125,793	130,859	135,675	139,722
455	100,082	113,230	128,334	140,255	139,699
2,691	592,037	621,639	646,505	665,900	754,464
990	217,800	224,334	231,064	237,996	245,136
1,202	264,545	272,481	280,656	289,075	297,747
250	55,000	55,000	55,000	55,000	55,000
7,747	**1,929,520**	**2,004,799**	**2,078,446**	**2,149,602**	**2,274,708**
	$1,406,557	**$1,769,543**	**$2,199,361**	**$2,525,573**	**$2,533,636**
	11.7%	25.8%	24.3%	14.8%	0.3%
	949,465	1,096,403	1,170,896	1,249,500	1,249,500
	1.48x	1.61x	1.88x	2.02x	2.03x
	270,050	270,050	270,050	270,050	270,050
	187,041	403,089	758,415	1,006,023	1,014,086
	756,000	604,800	403,200	268,800	342,200
			146,405		33,152,622
	$943,041	**$1,007,889**	**$1,308,020**	**$1,274,823**	**$34,508,908**

The main point here is that the property itself may not be distressed; it is the sponsor who is experiencing financial distress. Sure, many of the properties in real estate syndication deals were built in the 1980s and 1990s, and all the interiors need to be gutted. Perhaps the tenant base needs to be replaced. But, more often than not, the distress is not at the property level; it is at the sponsor level. The sponsor themselves could be distressed financially, perhaps because they do not have the right operational team in place or two partners had a falling out. In my role, I mitigate the likelihood that investors invest with a sponsor likely to become distressed.

WHO ARE THE KEY PLAYERS IN A REAL ESTATE SYNDICATION DEAL?

I introduced earlier what I consider the best analogy for a commercial real estate syndication, which is to think of it as an airplane ride. There are pilots, passengers, flight attendants, air traffic controllers, mechanics, and more who all work together to get the plane safely to its destination.

A private equity syndication is much like this. The passive investors, sponsors, brokers, property managers, contractors, building maintenance, and more all share a vision to invest in and improve a particular asset. However, each person's role in the project is different.

Here are the key roles that come together to make a real estate syndication happen:
- Real estate broker
- Lender
- General partners (sponsor)
- Key principals
- Limited partners (passive investors)
- Property manager

The real estate broker is the person or team who identifies the property for sale, either as a listing or as an off-market opportunity (i.e., not publicly listed). Having a strong real estate broker is crucial as they are the main liaison between the buyer and the seller throughout the acquisition process.

The lender is the biggest money partner in a real estate syndication because they provide the loan for the property. The lender performs their own due diligence through underwriting and gets a separate appraisal to make sure the property is worth the value of the loan requested.

In the airplane analogy, neither the real estate broker nor the lender is aboard the plane. The lenders and the real estate brokers are like the companies servicing the airline; they have important roles in bringing the project to fruition, but they are not part of the purchasing entity, nor do they share in any of the returns.

The general partners synchronize with the real estate broker and lender to secure the loan and acquire the property in addition to managing the asset throughout the life of the project, which is why they are often also called the lead syndicators. The general partner is the pilot of the plane.

The general partnership team includes both the sponsors and the operators (sometimes, these are the same people). The sponsors are the ones signing on the dotted line for the loan and are often involved in the acquisition and underwriting processes.

The operators are generally responsible for managing the acquisition and for executing the business plan by overseeing the day-to-day operations. Operators guide the property manager and ensure that renovations are on schedule and within budget.

KEY PRINCIPALS

For a commercial loan, the sponsor is required to show a certain amount of personal liquidity. This reassures the lender that the sponsor can contribute additional personal capital to keep the property afloat if things were ever to go wrong. One or more key principals may be brought into the deal to help guarantee the loan if the sponsor's personal balance sheet is insufficient.

A real estate syndication's passive investors have no active role in the project. They simply invest their money in exchange for a share of the returns. Like the passengers on an airplane, they get to put their money in, sit back, and enjoy the ride.

Once the property has been acquired, the property and construction management team arguably becomes the most important partner in the project. The property manager and their team are the boots on the ground, executing the renovations according to the business plan. The property manager works closely with the sponsor to ensure the business plan is being followed and any unexpected surprises are addressed properly. In the airplane analogy, the property manager could be likened to the co-pilot.

In our **SYNDICATION OFFERINGS**, Starting Point Capital is an extension of the sponsor's team. Our main role is to lead investor relations, review the underwriting criteria, and help to raise the equity needed.

We serve as an advocate for investors by ensuring that the sponsors' projections are conservative, deals are structured favorably toward

> **SYNDICATION OFFERING:** The comprehensive document that provides detailed information about a specific real estate investment opportunity. The offering includes property details, financial projections, terms of the investment, and other relevant information for potential passive investors to review before making an investment decision.

> **EXIT STRATEGY:**
> The predetermined plan for selling or exiting the real estate investment. This strategy outlines the time frame and approach to sell the property, potentially realizing capital gains and completing the investment cycle.

investors, multiple EXIT STRATEGIES exist, capital will be preserved, and the investment has the best chance of meeting or exceeding expected projections.

After the property is acquired, we act as the liaison between the sponsor/operator team and the investors by providing updates, financial reports, and other important information between parties.

One of my roles as a contact for investors is to guide them and reassure them. Many individuals tend to be headline investors. "Hey, Jeremy, I read this in the *Wall Street Journal*," they tell me. Or, "I read this in *Time*." They read an article or hear something in the news that bodes badly for some aspect of real estate investing, and they panic.

What clients may not realize is that this type of news tends to be very specific to either an asset class or a geographic area. Commercial real estate is a huge sector with dozens of different asset classes, sponsors, geographies, and so forth. A news story could be referring to office space, retail, or senior living facilities. Office space and retail got decimated during COVID and, while office space is limping back, retail space has been on a bull run lately.

Multifamily, which is the focus of Starting Point Capital, is a boring, non-sexy, commercial real estate asset, but that makes it less of a roller coaster ride. Everybody has to live somewhere so, while some areas of commercial real estate were devastated by COVID, multifamily was minimally impacted.

Also, which markets are the headlines talking about? Whether we are talking about an A class, B class, or C class property, multifamily real estate investing is very different if you are in Columbus, Ohio versus Irvine, California. Irvine is oversupplied, and valuations are strained. In Columbus, multifamily is providing amazing returns because big companies like Intel, for example, are creating new jobs and pumping billions of dollars into the local economy.

My advice to investors is to take what you hear in the news with a grain of salt. It is not always the truth, depending upon the asset class we are talking about and the specific market. Turn off the news and take advice from those on the front lines. Assuming you are aligned with a best-in-class operator, there are opportunities to invest in all stages of the economic cycle.

JEREMY DYER

ASSESSING THE SPONSOR

A good sponsor will do the work in finding the deals for you. But that does not mean you do not need to examine the deals they present to you; you absolutely should. However, once you establish a relationship with a real estate sponsor, you then need to focus on vetting the deals.

Because you are investing in the sponsor's competency, let us talk about their team. As the investor, focus on their track record. How long have they been operating real estate syndication opportunities? Did they just start syndicating apartment buildings last year? Are they a team of two? Are they a team of 10? Are they a team of 200? What markets do they operate in? How have they weathered times of adversity such as the historic run-up in interest rates or the global financial crisis? Have they actioned a capital call in the past? Did they suspend distributions on any investments? Have you run a background check on the team?

A strong track record and experience are key indicators of a general partner's ability to deliver returns. Transparency and communication are essential for building trust and ensuring that the investors (limited partners) are informed and engaged in the investment process. Financial stability, ethical standards, and legal compliance protect limited partners from potential financial and reputational damage. Lastly, alignment in the investment strategy, risk management, and exit plans are critical to meeting limited partners' financial goals and investment timelines.

The following is a comprehensive list of things to look for when evaluating a sponsor. I created this list based upon my experience vetting sponsors and matching them with investors. Best practices and research indicate that these factors are closely correlated with investment success and reducing risk exposure.

1. EXPERIENCE AND TRACK RECORD

Evaluate the general partner's past performance in similar investments. A strong track record indicates expertise and the ability to navigate various market conditions.

The image below shows the track record of the sponsor for the Rise West Arlington opportunity in Dallas-Fort Worth, Texas through Starting Point Capital.

TRACK RECORD

Property	Units	Purchase Price	Equity Raise	Projected Returns IRR	Projected Returns EM	Projected Returns Hold Period	Actual Returns IRR	Actual Returns EM	Actual Returns Hold Period
Rise Melrose	96	$18.4M	$6.0M	21.4%	2.38x	60 months	84.8%	2.02x	14.0 months
Scottsdale 5th	59	$6.6M	$2.6M	12.68%	1.70x	60 months	54.5%	3.42x	34.0 months
Rise on Thomas	100	$14.2M	$5.3M	19.9%	2.26x	60 months	66.3%	1.86x	14.0 months
Rise on Peoria	164	$28.7M	$9.1M	20.3%	2.30x	60 months	132.2%	2.45x	14.0 months
Rise Downtown Mesa	103	$16.5M	$6.1M	21.5%	2.39x	60 months	115.2%	2.26x	14.0 months
Rise Metro	160	$24.3M	$9.2M	17.2%	2.01x	60 months	108.6%	2.45x	14.0 months
Paseo 51	116	$15.5M	$4.9M	20.3%	2.25x	60 months	198.6%	3.85x	15.0 months
Villa Serena	137	$17.6M	$5.8M	19.0%	2.17x	60 months	65.4%	3.00x	27.0 months
Rise on McDowell	76	$6.9M	$3.7M	18.42%	2.15x	60 months	62.0%	2.90x	27.0 months
District Flats	112	$13.0M	$5.2M	19.3%	2.22x	60 months	83.7%	1.95x	13.5 months
Silver Oaks	36	$3.5M	$1.3M	13.6%	1.78x	60 months	44.6%	1.91x	18.0 months
**Total	Wtd. Avg.**	**1,159**	**$165.1M**	**$59.0M**	**19.30%**	**2.21x**	**60 months**	**103.50%**	**2.53x**	**17.7 months**

All Return Metrics Listed are Project Level Returns

2. MARKET KNOWLEDGE

The sponsor should have deep knowledge of the market where the investment is located. The sponsor should understand local demand, supply, and the regulatory environment. But it is not just familiarity with the economics that is important, it is familiarity and strong relationships with the local players.

Does the sponsor have leverage with the broker community? If they do, they can execute much more competitive deals. Many deals trade hands and never become public. The local brokers have relationships with all the owners whether the owners are institutional, syndication, or individual mom-and-pops. The brokers know who owns the properties, and they have regular conversations with those property owners. The best-in-class sponsors can leverage their relationships with brokers and find off-market deals. Because there are no competitors going after the same asset, the price may be lower.

What is the incentive for the broker to do an off-market deal? The brokers know that best-in-class sponsors offer an assurance of closing. Many sponsors will bid on different opportunities to stress the market. They might not have any intention of moving forward with the property. Rather, they have an eye on a particular asset and want to find out what it is worth to further understand where properties are trading in a particular market. To do that, they are often going to underwrite hundreds of deals and make offers on several properties.

Also, not every sponsor can raise the money to buy an asset. A sponsor might have an apartment building under contract for $30 million and not be able to raise the $14 million it needs from their limited partner investors. That may mean they cannot move forward with the transaction. They might lose their earnest money, or they might have to retrade. A retrade means that they ask for a concession on the sales price, say, from $30 million to $28 million. As you can probably gather, a broker would much rather work with a sponsor that they know has a higher assurance of closing and is not having to retrade because they cannot source the capital to acquire the asset.

3. INVESTMENT STRATEGY

Ensure the sponsor's investment strategy aligns with your risk tolerance, investment horizon, and financial goals.

4. FINANCIAL STABILITY

A sponsor with strong financial health is better positioned to weather economic downturns and has less need to rely solely upon limited partner capital.

5. TRANSPARENCY

The general partner should be open about the investment's financial aspects, risks, and operational status, providing regular, detailed reports.

6. COMMUNICATION

Effective and regular communication is key to trust and understanding and to ensuring that limited partners are informed and engaged. The sponsor should take the time to understand your goals and expectations.

7. LEGAL AND REGULATORY COMPLIANCE

Check if the sponsor has a clean record of adhering to legal and regulatory requirements to protect the investment from potential legal issues.

8. FEES AND COMPENSATION STRUCTURE

Understand how the sponsor is compensated to ensure it aligns with your interests and is fair relative to industry standards.

9. DUE DILIGENCE PROCESS

How does the sponsor select properties? Understand their due diligence process regarding the financing and the physical and legal inspections.

10. ASSET MANAGEMENT CAPABILITIES

Does the sponsor have a proven ability to manage properties effectively? What is their record regarding operational efficiency and tenant satisfaction?

11. RISK MANAGEMENT

What strategies does the sponsor use to mitigate investment risks, including market, financial, and operational risks?

12. EXIT STRATEGY

Does the sponsor have a clear, realistic plan for exiting the investment? Does it align with your investment horizon?

13. REPUTATION

Does the sponsor have a good reputation in the industry? Have you seen feedback from other investors and partners?

14. CO-INVESTMENT

Is the sponsor a CO-INVESTOR? Sponsors who invest with limited partners demonstrate confidence in the investment and, in this scenario, it is more likely that everyone's interests will align.

15. ETHICAL STANDARDS

Does the sponsor adhere to high ethical standards? For example, is the capital stack transparent and clearly communicated to the investor?

CO-INVESTMENT: An investment made jointly by multiple investors in a project. In real estate syndications, it can refer to a situation where the sponsor invests their own capital alongside investors.

16. OPERATIONAL EFFICIENCY

How does the sponsor operate properties, reduce costs, and increase profitability?

17. INNOVATION AND ADAPTABILITY

Does the sponsor show an ability to innovate and adapt to changing market conditions to protect and enhance investment value?

18. NETWORKING AND RELATIONSHIPS

Does the sponsor have good relationships with brokers, lenders, and other real estate professionals? These networks are advantageous when sourcing and managing investments.

19. TEAM AND EXPERTISE

Evaluate the experience and expertise of the sponsor's team. Do they have the skills necessary to manage the investment?

20. INVESTOR REFERENCES

Seek out current or past investors to hear their experience working with the sponsor.

21. CONFLICT OF INTEREST POLICIES

Does the sponsor have policies in place to manage conflicts of interest fairly?

22. TECHNOLOGY USE

Does the sponsor use the latest or recommended technology for property management, investor reporting, and market analysis?

23. PORTFOLIO DIVERSIFICATION

How does the investment fit within the sponsor's overall portfolio? Look at the levels of diversification and risk.

24. ALIGNMENT OF VALUES

Does your investment philosophy align with the sponsor's approach and culture? When you first meet or interview a sponsor, notice if they are interested in you. Do they ask what your goals and objectives are? If they do not, that is a red flag because they should want to make sure that the investment is the right one for you. Please refer to the appendix for a list of Starting Point Capital's sponsor evaluation criteria.

When considering a sponsor's track record, look at their brand reputation. A company that has a brand will not want to risk their reputation in a space where word-of-mouth is everything.

For accredited investors investing in advertised 506(c) offerings, a pre-existing relationship is not necessary but having a relationship with the sponsors you invest with is still a good idea whether or not it is required.

Invest in offerings in which the sponsor has experience. Look at their acquisition profile. If all their experience consists of, for example, buying 100-unit properties in Denver for $8 million to $10 million, be suspicious if the deal they are currently offering is 300 units in Seattle for $50 million.

I cannot stress enough the importance of underwriting hundreds of deals to learn the local market. When evaluating a sponsor and a deal, stress test the financials by looking at the TRAILING 12 MONTHS (TTM).

The TTM is a look back at the last 12 months of revenues, expenses, and net operating income. It shows the recent performance of an operator. Look for red flags. For example, are there any months where expenses were exorbitantly higher? If so, why was that the case? If you look at last year's TTM versus this year's TTM, was there a 30 percent increase in insurance costs? Did labor costs drastically increase? Did material costs drastically increase?

It is important that a sponsor underwrite hundreds of deals because there is no better way for a sponsor to really understand the local market. I would be nervous if a sponsor were only underwriting a dozen deals in a local market before they decided to take an opportunity under contract.

> **TRAILING 12 MONTHS (TTM):** A term that describes the past 12 consecutive months of a company's performance. The data gives a more current picture of a business's financial performance than its annual filings and reports, which, at times, can contain information that is more than a year old.

Get to know the sponsor and the team. Visit the sponsor's office if you can. Depending upon where they are located, it might be time-consuming, but it is worthwhile meeting the team face-to-face and seeing how they operate.

How is the company structured? Is it a company at all? Yes, there are individual syndicators out there. I am sure some are very successful; they just never found the need to create a cohesive team and a brand. But the most active groups know that having a solid management team, as well as a brand, is vitally important for long-term success. Syndicator teams are all structured differently. Some have external "partners" or "advisers" who may not have a full stake in the project. The more roles a sponsor takes on its own auspices, the less risk.

You will also find syndicators that operate with various joint venture partners or a "student army" consisting of beginners that the syndicator "mentors." These syndicators may partner with whoever brings the next deal or brings them investors. Each deal might have a variety of different players in the game. The result? There is a lack of focus as a team, so individuals have a watered-down stake in the global outcome.

ASSESSING THE DEAL

I have impressed upon you the importance of choosing the right sponsor, and I have warned against being swayed by a flashy pitch deck. So, how do you assess the deal and read between the lines of the investment summary?

The investment summary is a section of the confidential PRIVATE PLACEMENT MEMORANDUM (PPM) that quickly and as briefly as possible summarizes the real estate investment opportunity.

Deal sponsors put together investment summaries to explain to potential real estate investors why the deal is so great, what they plan to do with it, and how much passive income the investors stand to gain from participating in the investment.

PRIVATE PLACEMENT MEMORANDUM (PPM): A legal document stating the objectives, risks, and terms of an investment involved with a private placement. This document contains details about the investment property or portfolio.

As a discerning investor, you need to set aside your initial impressions—some executive summaries consist of gorgeous graphics, iconography, professional photos of the real estate project, and clear tables reflecting the projected returns. Others look like your Aunt Ida's tax returns replete with tea stains.

Although every investment summary is different, there are some basic elements that are pretty common across all multifamily real estate syndication investment summaries:
- Project name (often the name of the apartment complex)
- Photos of the rental property and area
- Overview of the submarket
- Overview of the deal
- Details of the business plan
- Projected returns and exit strategies
- Detailed numbers and analyses
- Team bios

Using the Rise West Arlington summary from our project in Texas, I will explain some of the more important things to look for.

What should stand out for you as the investor is that the structure of ownership is clearly laid out and transparent. It explains how you fit into the play of things and how the fund and sponsors are compensated.

PORFOLIO WITH LTV

Property	Acquisition Date	Purchase Price	Loan Amount	LTV at Acquisition
Rise at the Preserve	21-Jun	26,726,000	20,044,500	75.0%
Rise Biltmore	21-Jul	32,275,000	23,114,000	71.6%
Rise Desert West	21-Jul	41,600,000	31,200,000	75.0%
Rise Camelback	21-Aug	33,975,000	25,482,000	75.0%

THE FUNDAMENTAL INVESTOR

Property	Acquisition Date	Purchase Price	Loan Amount	LTV at Acquisition
Rise Parkside	21-Oct	56,075,000	42,000,000	74.9%
Rise at the Retreat	21-Oct	45,000,000	32,710,000	72.7%
Rise Skyview	21-Nov	62,315,000	46,800,000	75.1%
Rise Midtown	21-Dec	51,000,000	38,330,000	75.2%
Rise Westgate	21-Dec	32,300,000	24,325,000	75.3%
Rise Thunderbird	21-Dec	48,000,000	36,240,000	75.5%
Rise on Cave Creek	21-Dec	36,600,000	27,170,000	74.2%
Rise at Estrella Park	22-Jan	59,800,000	43,920,000	73.4%
Rise at the Lofts	22-Jan	25,200,000	17,987,000	71.4%
Rise Trailside	22-Mar	14,750,000	10,825,000	73.4%
Rise North Ridge	22-Mar	31,700,000	23,260,000	73.4%
Rise on Country Club	22-Mar	60,625,000	42,437,000	70.0%
Rise Canyon West	22-Mar	31,020,000	23,265,000	75.0%
Rise North Mountain	22-Apr	28,600,000	16,599,000	58.0%
Rise at Dobson Ranch	22-Apr	38,125,000	28,693,000	75.3%
Rise at the Palms	22-May	35,000,000	25,550,000	73.0%
Rise Broadway	22-May	92,000,000	65,726,242	71.4%
Rise at The District	22-May	142,000,000	97,172,000	68.4%
Rise Lakeside	22-Jun	75,300,000	51,327,500	68.2%
Rise Encore	22-Jul	125,000,000	79,375,000	63.5%
Rise at the Meadows	22-Sep	29,200,000	15,279,000	52.3%
Rise on Cactus	22-Sep	31,000,000	17,536,000	56.6%
Rise Suncrest	22-Nov	50,000,000	30,000,000	60.0%
Rise on McClintock	23-Jan	26,500,000	16,165,000	61.0%
Rise at Highland Meadows	23-Feb	NDS*	NDS*	56.1%
Rise Desert Cove	23-Mar	42,000,000	25,620,000	61.0%

Property	Acquisition Date	Purchase Price	Loan Amount	LTV at Acquisition
Rise Bedford Lake	23-Apr	NDS*	NDS*	65.0%
Rise Oak Creek	23-May	NDS*	NDS*	70.8%
Rise North Arlington	23-Jul	NDS*	NDS*	56.5%
Rise Creekside	23-Aug	NDS*	NDS*	65.0%
Rise Heather Ridge	23-Oct	NDS*	NDS*	55.9%
Rise Skyline	23-Nov	NDS*	NDS*	62.4%
Rise at Town East	23-Dec	NDS*	NDS*	55.6%
Rise Spring Pointe	24-Feb	NDS*	NDS*	57.2%
Rise Fossil Creek	24-Apr	NDS*	NDS*	70.0%

*NDS. This means that they were purchased in a non-disclosure state. Texas is NDS, so the state doesn't require sales price information to be provided to third parties. We don't post these because we could be subject to higher property taxes if disclosed.

LOAN-TO-VALUE (LTV) RATIO: A measure used by lenders to assess the risk of a loan. It is calculated by dividing the mortgage amount by the appraised property value.

The slide above details the operating team's track record. Clearly, this is not their first rodeo. The summary shows they have completed other successful projects with assets nearby. This implies that they have likely built up a strong reputation in the area among brokers, property managers, and other apartment owners.

Other track record details reveal a robust portfolio of properties and projects, including loan-to-value data such as the **LOAN-TO VALUE RATIO** (LTV).

The property, in this case, was purchased off-market directly from a distressed seller who is selling for a loss. This implies that the property was bought below market price and there is significant value-add upside for the property after the renovations.

DALLAS FORT WORTH QUICK FACTS

STRONG POPULATION GROWTH
Dallas-Fort Worth ranked #1 in the US for population growth from 2021-2022. Dallas is the 9th most populous city in the United States (US Census Bureau).

RENT GROWTH
Fort Worth has negative -1.67% effective rent growth from Q4 2022 to Q4 2023 (RealPage Analytics).

STRONG PROJECTED OCCUPANCY
Occupancy is slated to remain around 93.2% due to the supply / demand dynamics in the Arlington Metro area (Real Page).

MEDIAN SALES PRICE
The Median Sale Price of a single-family home in this Arlington area code is now $293K (Redfin.com, January 2024).

STRONG JOB GROWTH
Dallas – Fort Worth ranked #2 for job growth in the US in 2022 (US Bureau of Labor Statistics).

STRONG LABOR GROWTH
Dallas added over 242,000+ new jobs in 2022 (US Bureau of Labor Statistics).

The fact that Dallas-Fort Worth is ranked number one for population growth and number two for job growth implies a robust economy. The investment summary also gives details on the major employers in the area (Charles Schwab, Lockheed Martin, Kimberly Clark, Fidelity Investments, AT&T, and Southwest Airlines) and profiles on the various industry sectors.

2023 DALLAS RENOVATIONS

In 2023, we renovated 262 units across the Dallas portfolio with an average rental increase of $261. On average, this was $39 above our projected rents.

	2023*
Total Units Renovated	262
Average rental increase per unit	$261
Average rent over pro-forma	$39/unit

RENTAL INCREASE

■ Expected Pro-Forma Rent   ■ Actual Rent

Jackpot! A proven model takes all the guesswork and assumptions out of the value-add proposal. This slide shows that the previous operator already created the proof of concept. The operator updated a set amount of units and could fetch higher rents. This means that all the sponsor has to do is go in and repeat the same renovation plan to achieve those same rental increases. To me, this signals much lower risk in a value-add opportunity.

Another tool to use when assessing a project is a sensitivity analysis. A real estate sensitivity analysis assesses how different variables, such as rent growth, vacancy rates, interest rates, or operating expenses, impact the financial performance of an investment. By adjusting these inputs, investors can see how changes affect key metrics like cash flow, return on investment (ROI), and net operating income (NOI).

Such an analysis is crucial in passive real estate investing because it helps investors understand potential risks and ensure that their investment can withstand unfavorable conditions, providing a clearer picture of the range of possible outcomes.

EQUITY MULTIPLE

	Investor Returns
IRR	16.4–16.9%
Equity Multiple	2.05–2.09x
Avg. Cash Flow	5.2%
Annualized Returns	21.0–21.9%

Equity Member – Sample $100,000 Investment		
LP - Equity Member	Investment	**Total Return**
Cash Flow %		
Cash Flow*	($100,000)	**$26,244**
Return on sale	$0	**$178,617**
Total Return	**($100,000)**	**$204,861**

LP - Equity Member	Year 1	Year 2	Year 3	Year 4	Year 5
Cash Flow %	3.8%	4.2%	5.9%	5.9%	6.6%
Cash Flow*	$3,770	$4,178	$5,869	$5,856	$6,571
Return on sale	$0	$0	$0	$0	$178,617
Total Return	**$3,770**	**$4,178**	**$5,869**	**$5,856**	**$185,188**

The equity multiple is important. In this case, the projected equity multiple is 2.05x to 2.09x. This means that, during the life of this project, your money will more than double. That is, if you were to invest $100,000 of your hard-earned money, you would come out of this project with $205,000.

This $205,000 - $209,000 return on and return of capital would include your original $100,000 investment as well as $105,000 of your monthly distributions and profit participation. This $105,000 includes the monthly or quarterly cash-on-cash returns you should receive while the asset is held as well as your portion of the profits when the asset is sold.

Aim for an equity multiple of around 2x, but do not chase deals that offer the best projected returns as those are merely projections.

This is a 220-unit multifamily investment opportunity. Projects of over 100 units bring economies of scale and increasing efficiencies by leveraging shared resources. In addition, this project takes advantage of the sponsor's resources and materials in another location: Phoenix, Arizona. This sponsor has a consistent supply chain, which stabilizes material costs and leverages a reduction in cost due to purchasing power.

You have to move quickly if you like what you see. As I mentioned, this opportunity in Texas filled up within hours. Be ready to make a soft commitment to reserve your spot, and then take time to review the investment summary in detail.

There is no penalty for backing out of a real estate investment before the funding deadline, so it is to your benefit to reserve early to ensure you get a spot in the deal.

JEREMY DYER

FINDING CAPITAL FOR REAL ESTATE SYNDICATION

If I have done my job right, and this book is doing what it is supposed to, you are thinking seriously about investing passively in real estate. If so, you might be asking, "How can I find the capital to invest passively in real estate syndication?"

My advice? First, pay off your high-interest debt. There is no point in making returns of 16 percent when you are paying 22 percent in credit card debt. Second, invest for delayed gratification rather than spending now to relieve momentary dissatisfaction.

The obvious sources of capital are cash that you might have on hand or in low-interest rate savings accounts. You could also liquidate stock and, as I have already argued, passive real estate investments have historically outperformed Wall Street. You could also use a HELOC if you have equity in your home, and you could borrow against your 401(k) or use old 401(k) dollars to invest through a self-directed IRA. Again, I would advise you to talk to your CPA to see how your taxes might be affected by whichever strategy you choose.

I will be honest. If you spend more money than you make, you will not find the capital. But, by living with fewer luxuries and enjoying simpler pleasures, it is entirely possible to get your financial house in order so that you can invest. The following are some less obvious ways to raise capital and, if you think outside the box, you will find more.

I believe that most people could, if they were really purposeful about their saving and spending habits, save an additional $10,000 per year. Higher net worth individuals could probably find a way to save $100,000 more per year—perhaps they do not need the Escalade, and they could get by with the Ford Explorer.

Rather than spending $100,000 dollars on the Escalade, why not put that $100,000 to work in a passive investment that produces a seven or eight percent cash-on-cash return on an annual basis? Before you know it, you can use the cash flow from your investment to pay for the loan on your Escalade.

Think creatively. My father owned a boat slip on the St. Croix River in Minnesota. Around 10 years ago, he was thinking about selling his boat slip. Because the river is a nationally protected riverway, no new supply of slips could be introduced, so I knew that the ones that remained were going to be in demand.

"Dad," I asked him one day, "why would you sell your boat slip when other people will pay a premium in the future to rent it? It has got significant cash flow and long-term appreciation potential."

My father was adamant that he wanted to sell it, so I purchased the boat slip from him for $85,000. Today, I could sell it for $225,000, and I regularly get offers from people to buy it. In addition to its increasing value, the boat slip provides cash flow. I do not have a boat in it. I just own the slip, so I rent it out for $12,000 a year.

Lots of high net worth people have RVs, boats, trailers, motor homes, and cabins. They could potentially rent these out. Marlene and I own a 40-foot RV. It sleeps up to 10 people. We rent it out for anywhere between $550 and $700 per night. It is insane to me that people are willing to pay that much money to rent an RV. One summer, someone rented it for 20 days for $600 per night. I earned $12,000 just to rent my RV for 20 days.

There was no cost to me for doing that. I have to pay insurance on the RV, anyway, and I would still have to pay a fee to park it when it is not in use. There were some miles added onto the chassis, but the chassis is good for a million miles, anyway, and I barely put 4,000 miles per year on it.

Do you own a boat or an RV? Do you own jet skis? Do you own a cabin? Do you have room for a lodger in your house? If you have an extra bedroom in your house, you could charge somebody $400 or $1,000 a month, depending upon where you live. That is all potential additional cash flow that you can use for passive investing.

As I mentioned before, a popular way to invest in real estate syndication opportunities is through a self-directed IRA. There are trillions of dollars in America locked up inside IRAs because, every time somebody changes a job, their active 401(k) gets rolled into an IRA.

Some people who contribute money to their IRA every year do so because their financial advisor tells them to. Those IRAs are growing by around four to seven percent per year and are just about keeping pace with inflation. In a good year, they might exceed the inflation rate slightly and, in a bad year, they might lag behind. One year, you might earn 12 percent and, the next, negative six percent.

Let us say you have $100,000 invested in the market, and it drops to $50,000. You have lost 50 percent. Now let us just say that your $50,000 investment increases 50 percent the following year. Are you back up to $100,000? The answer is no; you are only up to $75,000. Your money went up by 50 percent of $50,000, which is $25,000. So, you lost money even though the return percentage equaled out. When reviewing quarterly statements, people get this calculation wrong all the time.

An alternative option to consider is to set up an account with a self-directed IRA custodian. You can use that IRA money to invest in a passive real estate syndication where you can diversify and may see an outsized return from that of Wall Street. You cannot take IRA money from your Schwab account or your Fidelity account and invest it directly in one of our opportunities unless you have a custodian such as Custodians Equity Trust or Madison Trust.

The IRA custodian will move, however, as much as you want from your IRA to your self-directed IRA account. The self-directed IRA can be invested in a passive real estate investment. Self-directed IRAs can be used for many types of alternative investing. They are just a way to unshackle locked up capital.

A securities-based line of credit (SBL) is a way to borrow against non-retirement investment assets like stocks and bonds. Doing so can provide capital for investments without triggering capital gains taxes. There are some caveats, however, which include borrowing limits. You cannot borrow above 50 percent of your equities' value. If the market takes a turn, that could trigger a maintenance call, so you have to be a little careful. Monitor market conditions and plan to pay off loans if the market starts to shift.

If finding the funds to invest in a real estate syndication seems daunting, which it might because you typically need at least $50,000 to invest in a deal, perhaps I can allay your concerns in the next chapter by showing you how quickly you can see returns and the opportunities that exist for scaling.

V
THE RETURNS AND SCALING

The best news about real estate syndication is that there are plenty of opportunities for scaling. I tell my investors that there is no need for a scarcity mindset.

Marlene and I first invested in an opportunity in 2015, which was a multifamily project. After that one investment in 2015, we doubled our money by 2019 with no additional real estate investments as a passive investment during that four-year period. After seeing the returns, from 2019 to 2024, we invested in 29 more projects. We have diversified into self-storage, assisted living, flex office, and retail projects. There are plenty of other real estate projects to invest in outside of B-class value-add apartment buildings.

A scarcity mindset is a tendency to be protective over assets or another area in which they are involved. For example, a salesperson might be territorial and not want others to encroach upon their potential leads within a certain boundary.

When my children were younger, I watched them inevitably fight over toys. "That's mine! No, it's not, it's mine!" You get the picture. Sadly, the same thing happens with adults in the business world when, in reality, there is enough for everyone.

When I was in sales, I tried to maintain a mentality of abundance. There is plenty to go around, and there is no need for sandbox disputes. I found that giving to people was a much better strategy. Friends of mine would say, "Jeremy, you're competing against these people, but you're giving them business. You're giving them your playbook, your blueprint for success." Real estate syndication is a massive space, and there is room for everyone. There is room for scaling and for huge returns. Let us look a bit more closely at the scope for real estate investments.

Supply and demand are really the fundamentals of real estate 101. The National Multifamily Housing Council (NMHC) suggested that we have to build 4.3 million more apartment units as a nation between now and 2035 to keep up with the demand for multifamily housing or for rental housing in general. Meanwhile, builders have scaled back to the tune of 40 to 50 percent on new permits and new starts for new construction. So, we are already behind, and builders are scaling back massively. Where does that put you as an investor or owner in five years? There is a supply-demand imbalance right now with lots of demand coming in and little supply. I believe multifamily investors are going to be very thankful in five years that they made investments today.

Also, we have the largest gap in United States history between a new mortgage payment and apartment rents. That gap is nearly $1,000 per month, and that is just the principal and interest payment. As a homeowner, you might have homeowners' association dues, property taxes, much higher insurance, maintenance, upkeep, rehab, and so forth. It is super expensive to be a homeowner right now, making multifamily investing an excellent option for those looking to diversify into quality cash-flowing assets.

> Investing passively in real estate is not a get-rich-quick scheme. It is not about timing the market; it is about spending time in the market.

That said, investing passively in real estate is not a get-rich-quick scheme. It is not about timing the market; it is about spending time in the market.

Once you get started with passive real estate investing, you begin to receive cash flow from your investments, and you gain some tax benefits, but it starts to get really exciting when you exit deals. That is when you can start to scale.

When you exit a deal with a profit, you can redeploy or recycle that capital into the next deal. The expectation is that these investments will double every three to five years. That is your 2x equity multiple. With this equity multiple, three to five years out, if your initial investment was $50,000, that investment will be at least $100,000. You redeploy that $100,000 into another deal with a three- to five-year hold period, and now that becomes $200,000. In another three to five years, your initial investment of $50,000 will grow to $400,000 and then $800,000 and then $1.6 million.

And that is just after one $50,000 investment. Most higher net worth individuals could manage a $50,000 or $100,000 investment three or four times a year. They can really stack up and compound their investments. So, you can see how things can scale quickly.

I like to use marathon running as an analogy. I have run 20 marathons in the Midwest. However, the wear and tear on my body, getting up at 4 a.m. on Saturday mornings to get in a 20-miler, needing time afterwards to clear the mental fog and perhaps taking a nap was not sustainable for the long term. Nevertheless, if your goal is to run 26.2 miles, you train up to it over a set period, run your race, and then recover.

Training is going to take time. It also takes time for your investments in passive real estate investing to show returns. Think about each $50,000 investment as five miles invested into your marathon training. Each five miles takes your body to another level. Over time, the miles stack up as your body becomes fitter and stronger.

Similarly, your investments produce regular, consistent cash flow distributions paid monthly or quarterly. Just like your body builds strength during your early miles, you are reaping some benefit immediately from early investments in the form of distributions.

It is not easy to live off dividends from dividend-paying stocks because, in most cases, those dividends are hardly enough to change your financial situation. They might pay a dividend of five percent annually. The problem with dividend-paying stock is that, yes, you might be getting a nice dividend, but the stock may not have moved in 25 years.

There is also an end goal with a marathon. It is to complete 26.2 miles and to reach the finish line. With investing, the finish line is quitting your day job and stepping off the hamster wheel. It is becoming a corporate refugee and replacing your W2 with cash-flowing passive income. If you are earning $300,000 a year, how many of these $50,000 investments—over what time period—will get you to the point where you are financially free, which simply means a point where your passive income equals or exceeds your active earned income?

The more investments you make, the more quickly you can get to the finish line, but therein lies the challenge for most people. That is because freeing up the cash for additional investments will require adjusting your lifestyle, something that few people want to do. Most people want to maintain their current lifestyle or even improve it, particularly high net worth individuals. I think it is a misconception that most people will scale down their expenses when they retire. Who really wants to get to retirement age and then, all of a sudden, stop living life because they do not have enough cash flow?

Also, consider inflation. A dollar today is not the same value as a dollar tomorrow. Not long from now, the price of today's $150 ticket to Disney World will be closer to $250.

JEREMY DYER

THE KEY STEPS OF PASSIVE REAL ESTATE INVESTING

What I have just explained is a 10,000-foot level overview of the reasons I started my company, Starting Point Capital, and why high net worth individuals invest in real estate syndication through my company.

Investing passively in real estate syndication can be a powerful way to build wealth, but it requires due diligence, understanding the process, and sometimes a significant investment. Here are the key steps involved.

1. EDUCATE YOURSELF

Before diving into real estate syndication, educate yourself on what it entails. Understand the terms, how returns are generated, and the risks involved. Real estate syndication involves pooling money from multiple investors to buy properties that are typically larger, trade at a multiple of net operating income, and are more lucrative than properties one investor could afford on their own.

2. ASSESS YOUR FINANCIAL SITUATION

Evaluate your financial readiness to invest. Real estate syndications often require a minimum investment and a long-term commitment, usually three to five years or more. Ensure you have enough liquidity and that your investment aligns with your overall financial goals.

3. FIND AND VET SYNDICATIONS

Look for real estate syndication opportunities, which can be found through networks, investment groups, or online platforms specializing in real estate investments. Once you find a potential investment, thoroughly vet the syndication by researching the company's track record, the property in question, the market it operates in, and the terms of the deal.

4. REVIEW LEGAL DOCUMENTS

Once you decide to move forward with an investment, you will receive a private placement memorandum, an operating agreement, and a subscription agreement. These documents outline the terms of the investment, the structure of the deal, the risks, and your rights. As an investor, it is crucial to review these documents carefully, preferably with the help of a legal advisor.

The sponsor or syndicator is the party responsible for identifying, acquiring, managing, and eventually selling the property. Conducting due diligence on the sponsor's experience, reputation, and past performance is crucial for assessing the potential success of the investment.

5. COMMIT TO YOUR INVESTMENT

If everything checks out and you decide to proceed, you will commit your capital by signing the subscription agreement and wiring your investment funds to the designated account.

6. ONGOING MANAGEMENT AND COMMUNICATION

After investing, your role becomes relatively passive. The sponsor handles the day-to-day management of the investment. However, you should receive regular updates on the property's performance, including financial statements and updates on any significant developments, returns, and exits.

Understand how and when you will receive returns. These can come from operational cash flows, (e.g., rental income) and the eventual sale of the property. Be clear about the projected holding period and the strategy for exiting the investment.

Investing in real estate syndications offers the opportunity to participate in larger, potentially more profitable deals than individual investments. However, it is essential to approach these opportunities with a thorough understanding and due diligence to mitigate risks and align with your investment goals.

DRAWING OUTSIDE THE LINES

If you are a parent, you will likely agree that a lot of what we do is based upon a desire to provide as best we can for our children. Also, I would be lying if I said I do not want my kids to consider me a cool dad. I want my kids to want to follow in my footsteps, but I also want them to think outside of the box and make their own mistakes. I realize that the world is changing and that what I did in life is not necessarily what they should do. That is why experimenting with new ideas is crucial.

My older children are now on their second or third round of entrepreneurial ventures (which I have seed funded, of course), and I am trying desperately to be hands-off (operationally).

A few years ago, my children and I started up a coffee roasting business called StirStix Coffee. This was the natural progression from the omnipresent lemonade stand. Making lemonade out of lemons, while perhaps profitable in August in hot Georgia, is not going to do well in the sub-zero climate of Minnesota.

So, a coffee roasting business it was. We bought a commercial coffee roaster for $14,000, and my two older boys were sent out to find sales either door-to-door or through a retailer. We developed a logo and set up a website. I told my children that, if they paid off the startup costs within three years, including the coffee roaster, we could call that a home run. Well, they paid it off in two years.

After a good run, we recently shut the business down because I felt they had learned all the lessons they needed from that venture—they learned the sales, accounting, and service side of the business and, frankly, Marlene and I were doing most of the back-end work.

The next chapter for my children is an outdoor lawn services company. We have acquired the equipment, and my oldest son now has a license so that he can buy and drive a truck and trailer. They still need mentorship and guidance, but I am letting them make their own mistakes. With the lawn services business, they are managing the whole business life cycle.

Not all my children are business or sales oriented. They are all different. My youngest son is engineering minded and reads books constantly. My oldest son would not dream of opening a book unless he had to, but he would listen to an audiobook. I am letting them follow their instincts because raising children according to their bent is a biblical concept, which is important to me.

In the same way, all investors with Starting Point Capital are different. They have their own reasons for wanting to passively invest in real estate syndication, and they all have different prior investing experiences. I can help guide them. However, the real learning comes when they invest in their first opportunity, and their experiences make them more discerning and more qualified to make more informed investment decisions in the future.

When I jumped into real estate syndication, the fact that I was eschewing Wall Street mores and scripts and taking a potentially riskier path did not faze me. I have been drawing outside the lines all my life. The traditional investing advice bored me, and the results were far from impressive.

While I am not a supporter of Hollywood movies and their sensationalist scripts and scenes, the following excerpt from the screenplay of the movie *Wolf of Wall Street* says it all. The story of the actual wolf of Wall Street and his mentor Mark Hanna is real, and the movie exposes the unscrupulous and even nebulous entity that is Wall Street and the stock markets.

Mark Hanna: Number one rule of Wall Street. Nobody—and I don't care if you're Warren Buffet or if you're Jimmy Buffet—nobody knows if a stock is going to go up, down, sideways, or in circles. You know what a fugazi is?

Jordan Belfort: Fugayzi, it's a fake.

Mark Hanna: Fugayzi, fugazi. It's a whazy. It's a woozie. It's fairy dust. It doesn't exist. It's never landed. It is no matter. It's not on the elemental chart. It's not f***ing real.

That is how I feel about Wall Street and stocks.

We live in a different world today where the news we receive is often biased. Growing up, I was taught to view the media with caution—believing that it can often be more of an enemy than an ally to the people. While the media plays a crucial role in informing the public, there is no denying that it can also be manipulated and driven by agendas that do not always align with the truth.

Today, it is more important than ever to approach the news with a critical eye. Media corruption, whether through selective reporting, sensationalism, or outright misinformation, can distort reality and mislead the public. We must be vigilant in questioning what we are told, seeking out diverse sources, and thinking critically about the information we consume.

In a world where narratives can be shaped by those in power, caution is not just advisable—it is essential. The truth is out there, but it is up to us to find it amidst the noise.

Lastly, I would like to talk less about you as an investor and more about you as a person. It is often said that we are the average of the five people we spend the most time with. While this might sound like a cliché, there is profound truth behind it: The people you surround yourself with and the voices you choose to listen to or read will inevitably shape who you become.

The people in your life—whether friends, family, colleagues, or mentors—play a significant role in shaping your thoughts, attitudes, and behaviors. If you are surrounded by individuals who are driven, positive, and successful, their energy and mindset will naturally rub off on you. On the other hand, if your circle is filled with negativity, complacency, or a lack of ambition, it is likely that these attitudes will start to influence you.

Think about it: If you spend your time with people who constantly push their limits, set ambitious goals, and strive for growth, you will be inspired to do the same. Their success becomes a mirror for your own potential, encouraging you to reach higher. Conversely, if you are surrounded by those who are content with mediocrity or who constantly complain without taking action, it is easy to fall into the same patterns.

In today's digital age, the people you listen to are not just those in your immediate physical circle. They also include the books you read, the podcasts you tune into, the social media accounts you follow, and the thought leaders you look up to. These voices are constantly feeding your mind with ideas, perspectives, and values that shape your worldview.

While these voices can serve as a source of inspiration, motivation, guidance, and growth, they can also promote negativity, fear, or a fixed mindset limiting your potential and keeping you stuck in a cycle of inaction.

Surround yourself with individuals who are aligned with your goals, values, and vision for the future. Remember, the people and voices you allow into your life are powerful influencers of your own trajectory. Choose wisely, and your future self will thank you for it.

My journey so far with passive investing has been a fascinating learning curve. I can tell you that passive investing in real estate syndications has surpassed my expectations, and I see no reason for that to change. People will always need housing, properties always need to be built or renovated, and the ups and downs of the business cycle can be managed if the deals are structured correctly and the operators know how to weather economic headwinds.

In short, it has been an exciting ride so far—and one I highly recommend.

COMMON QUESTIONS ABOUT PASSIVE REAL ESTATE INVESTING AND SYNDICATION OPPORTUNITIES

The same questions often come up when I am consulting with clients about investing in real estate syndications. Here is a list of the most common questions and my responses to them.

WHERE DO I FIND REAL ESTATE SYNDICATION OPPORTUNITIES?

The truth is, you will not unless you are tied in with the right networks. Public offerings are typically only for accredited investors, and Starting Point Capital cannot publicly advertise its syndication opportunities. Therefore, they are limited to friends and family or referrals through word of mouth. Your best bet is to start talking to other investors, attending networking events, and finding the right sponsors.

WHAT IS THE DIFFERENCE BETWEEN REITS AND REAL ESTATE SYNDICATIONS?

Real estate investment trusts (REITs) are easy to access, and many investors turn to publicly traded REITs to diversify their investment portfolios. When you invest in a REIT, you are purchasing or acquiring ownership shares in a company that invests in commercial real estate. Here are the differences between a REIT and a real estate syndication:

1. Number of Properties

A REIT will hold a portfolio of properties across multiple markets in an asset class, which could mean broad diversification for investors. Separate REITs are available for apartment buildings, shopping malls, office buildings, elderly care, and so on. With real estate syndications, you invest in a not-publicly-traded single asset property. You know the exact location, the number of units, the financials specific to that property, and the business plan for your investment. This may not be the case with a REIT.

2. Ownership

When investing in a REIT, you purchase publicly traded shares in the company that owns the real estate assets. When you invest in a real estate syndication, you and others contribute directly to the purchase of a specific property through the entity (usually an LLC) that holds the asset.

3. Access

Most REITs are listed on major stock exchanges, and you may invest in them directly through mutual funds or via exchange-traded funds quickly and easily online. Real estate syndications, on the other hand, are often under an SEC regulation that disallows public advertising. That means that you need to have a relationship with a sponsor or fund manager. Some opportunities are only open to accredited investors although that is not typically the case with Starting Point Capital.

4. Investment Minimums
REITs have very low minimum investments. A real estate syndication deal will typically require an investment of $50,000 or more.

5. Liquidity
At any time, you can buy or sell shares of your REIT. Your money is liquid and may or may not be worth what you originally acquired the shares for, and you most certainly can lose money based upon the volatility in the public markets. Real estate syndications, however, are accompanied by a business plan that often defines holding the asset for a certain amount of time (often three to five years) during which your money is locked in.

6. Tax Benefits
When you invest in a REIT, because you are investing in the company and not directly in physical real estate, you do not benefit from tax depreciation benefits. There are no tax breaks, and you will have no depreciation to offset any of your passive income.

When you invest directly in a property (real estate syndications included), you receive a variety of tax deductions with the main benefit being depreciation (i.e., writing off the value of an asset over time). Sometimes, the depreciation benefits surpass the cash flow, and you may show a loss on paper but have positive cash flow. Those paper losses can then be used to offset your passive income.

7. Returns
While returns for any real estate investment can vary wildly, the historical data over the last 40 years reflects an average of 12.87 percent per year in total returns for exchange-traded U.S. equity REITs. By comparison, stocks averaged 11.64 percent per year over that same period.

This means, on a historical average, if you invested $100,000 in a REIT, you could expect somewhere around $12,870 per year in dividends, which is a great ROI.

Between the cash flow and the profits from the sale of the asset, real estate syndications can offer around 20 percent average annual returns that are tax advantaged.

As an example, a $100,000 investment into a syndication with a five-year hold period and a 20 percent average annual return may average $20,000 per year for five years or $100,000 (this takes into account both cash flow and profits from the sale), which means that your money can double over the course of those five years.

WHAT IS THE RULE OF 72?

The Rule of 72 is a formula used to estimate the number of years required to double invested money at a given annual rate of return. The basic idea of the Rule of 72 is that if you take the number 72 and divide it by the annual rate of return, this will equal the number of years it takes for an investment to double. For example, if the investment target IRR is 16 percent, using the Rule of 72, you would expect to double your investment in approximately 4.5 years.

WHAT IS THE MINIMUM INVESTMENT REQUIRED FOR SYNDICATION REAL ESTATE?

The minimum investment for real estate syndication can vary widely, depending upon the deal and the syndicator, but it typically ranges from $25,000 to $100,000 or more. With Starting Point Capital, it is typically $50,000.

ARE REAL ESTATE SYNDICATIONS AVAILABLE FOR NON-ACCREDITED INVESTORS?

An accredited investor is a higher net worth individual that the SEC deems capable of absorbing the potential risks in the world of investing. A non-accredited investor is someone who does not meet the income or net worth requirements set out by the Securities and Exchange Commission (SEC). Starting Point Capital's opportunities are open to both accredited and non-accredited investors as are other real estate syndication opportunities.

HOW LONG IS THE TYPICAL INVESTMENT HORIZON IN REAL ESTATE SYNDICATION?

The investment horizon for real estate syndication can vary, but it typically ranges between three to five years, depending upon the project and the sponsor's business plan. Starting Point Capital's opportunities typically have a time horizon of three to five years.

CAN I INVEST IN SYNDICATED REAL ESTATE DEALS THROUGH RETIREMENT FUNDS OR A SELF-DIRECTED IRA?

Yes. Many of my clients at Starting Point Capital use their self-directed IRA to fund their investment. An IRA is typically deemed a safer investment but, currently, your money is only growing by around four to seven percent and barely keeping up with inflation. In a good year, your investment might beat inflation and, in the next, lag behind.

If you use a self-directed IRA, you will first need an IRA custodian such as Equity Trust, Custodians Equity Trust, or Madison Trust. Your IRA custodian can then move as much as you want to invest from your traditional or Roth IRA into a self-directed IRA account. The self-directed IRA account can then invest directly in one of our future real estate opportunities.

WHAT ARE THE TAX IMPLICATIONS OF INVESTING IN SYNDICATED REAL ESTATE DEALS?

I am not a tax professional. Therefore, the insights and perspectives I offer come from are my experience only. You should speak with your CPA for more details and specifics on your situation. That said, the tax implications of passive real estate investing are significant, which is why it is so appealing to the rich. I cover this topic in depth in Section II of the book, but here is a synopsis of the tax benefits of investing in a real estate syndication.

1. The tax code favors real estate investors.
The IRS recognizes that real estate investing provides quality housing for people to live in. Because of this important role, the tax code rewards real estate investors for investing in real estate, maintaining those units, and making upgrades over time. (Keep reading.)

2. As a passive investor, you benefit from the same tax benefits an active investor gets.
You are investing in real estate but, even though you are not actively fixing any toilets or climbing on any roofs, you still receive the same tax benefits by being a passive investor. This is because you invest in an entity that owns the property, and that entity is considered a pass-through entity. As such, the tax benefits flow right through that entity to you, the investor.

Common tax benefits from investing in real estate include being able to write off expenses related to the property (including things like repairs, utilities, payroll, and interest) as well as writing off the value of the property over time (this is called depreciation).

Contrast this with investing in a real estate investment trust (REIT). With a REIT, you are investing in a company, not directly in the underlying real estate. Therefore, you do not get the same tax benefits.

3. Depreciation is huge.
Depreciation is one of the most powerful wealth-building tools in real estate. Depreciation lets you write off the value of an asset over time, being based upon the wear and tear and the useful life of an asset. Real estate lasts a long time, so the IRS allows you to write off the value of the property over 27.5 years.

4. Cost segregation is depreciation on steroids.
Straight-line depreciation allows you to write off an equal amount of the value of the asset every year for 27.5 years. However, for most of the real estate syndications we invest in, the hold time is around five years. So, if we were to deduct an equal amount every year for 27.5 years, we would only get five years of those benefits. We would be leaving the remaining 22.5 years of depreciation benefits on the table. Cost segregation is a strategy that allows you to deconstruct

a property and identify components that can be depreciated over a shorter timeline—five, seven, or 15 years.

Note: Bonus depreciation rules that were enacted in 2017 through the Tax Cuts and Jobs Act allow the investor to take 100 percent of the depreciation immediately. This tax law started to be phased out in 2022 and, at the time of writing, sits at 60 percent bonus depreciation. Unless Congress enacts a new tax law change, the bonus percentage will continue to decrease by 20 percent each year until it eventually phases out completely in 2027.

5. Capital gains and depreciation recapture are things for which you should plan.

It is not all gains where taxes are concerned. When a property is sold, capital gains and depreciation recapture come into play. In a real estate syndication that holds a property for five years, you would not have to worry about capital gains taxes and depreciation recapture until the asset is sold in year five. The specific amount of capital gains and depreciation recapture depends upon the length of the hold time as well as your individual tax situation.

6. 1031 exchanges can help with capital gains taxes.

A 1031 exchange allows you to exit from investment property and, within a set amount of time, swap that asset for another like-kind investment property. If you exchange the asset within the allotted time frame, instead of having the profits paid out directly to you, you can roll them into the next investment. Then, you will not owe any capital gains when the first property is sold.

HOW DO I FIND EXPERIENCED SPONSORS AND EVALUATE THEIR TRACK RECORDS?

Hopefully, this book has given you a solid education in real estate syndication and how to evaluate a sponsor. Finding a sponsor is a matter of networking and building relationships with sponsors and fund managers. Section IV of this book explains the science behind real estate syndication, how the financing works, the risks to you as a limited partner, and how to evaluate the sponsor.

WHAT HAPPENS IF A SPONSOR OR A PROPERTY FAILS TO EXECUTE ITS BUSINESS PLAN?

I will not sugarcoat the risks. If a property underperforms, investors may experience negative repercussions, including losing some or all of their capital. The specific impact will depend upon the deal's structure and the reasons for the underperformance. Again, this underscores the importance of making sure that you have a sponsor leading the charge who knows what they are doing, has a best-in-class team, and has a solid track record.

CAN I EXIT A SYNDICATION REAL ESTATE DEAL BEFORE THE INVESTMENT TERM ENDS?

Exiting early can be challenging. However, some syndicators may offer buyout options or facilitate secondary sales, but these can come with challenges and potential discounts. It is up to you to find out the answers to these types of questions from the sponsor before you commit. If the answers are not clear, or the sponsor is less than transparent, consider that a red flag.

There are three options for selling shares early: Sell shares to the general partner, sell shares to other limited investor partners, or bring in a new investor who will buy your shares. The rules and any penalties should be addressed in the operating agreement. However, it is best to go into a syndication deal with the expectation that the money will be illiquid for the deal term.

ARE THERE ANY SPECIFIC LEGAL REQUIREMENTS FOR SYNDICATED REAL ESTATE INVESTMENTS?

Yes, real estate syndications must comply with various laws, and syndicators must provide detailed disclosure documents to potential investors. Compliance with local real estate laws and regulations is also essential. Private placement offerings are filed by the sponsor's attorney with the SEC, and Blue Sky filing notices are sent on behalf of the investor to the state in which the investor claims primary residence.

IS THERE SUCH A THING AS ONLINE REAL ESTATE SYNDICATION THROUGH A CROWDFUNDING PLATFORM?

Real estate syndication involves a collection of investors pooling resources to invest in property, typically managed by a sponsor. There are online real estate syndication platforms, often called real estate crowdfunding platforms, that connect investors to these opportunities, making investment more accessible. However, you will be limited in the way you interact with the sponsor, and evaluating the sponsors and the deal structures might be a challenge.

These platforms operate in one of two ways. In the first, the platform itself is the sponsor raising funds to be deployed in another operator's deal. You have no interaction with the operating partner actually managing the property, no prior relationship with the sponsor, and no way to materially vet them.

Lastly, the platform will charge fees, so your returns may not be as good as they might be if you invested directly with a reliable and more exclusive sponsor or through a company like Starting Point Capital.

The second way these platforms operate is as the connection point between you and the operating partner. With this scenario, you can vet the sponsor, but you still have to pay asset management fees.

WHEN DOES A PREFERRED RETURN START ACCRUING? DOES IT ROLL OVER?

If your deal shows a preferred return, when it starts to accrue will depend upon the deal structure. It could be on day one, or there might not be any cash flow for the first year or two. Will the preferred return roll over? For example, if a deal projecting an annual eight percent preferred return only delivers six percent in year one, what happens to the remaining two percent? Does it disappear or does it accrue to be made up in the subsequent years? Industry standard at the time of writing is for the preferred return to roll over or accrue until it is completely caught up.

WHEN WILL I GET MY FIRST DISTRIBUTION?

When you should expect your first distribution depends upon the type of deal and the business plan. Some projects are basic yield plays that start churning out cash from day one. Other projects requiring a value-add renovation plan could take upwards of six months or longer. Distributions might be monthly or quarterly, again depending upon the deal structure.

HAS YOUR MINDSET CHANGED? IF SO, IT'S TIME TO ACT

I hope I have succeeded in my goal to educate you, the reader, on a better way to invest. Passively investing in real estate syndications puts your money to work for you without using up your time. It creates cash flow today that you can use to build wealth for tomorrow. Investors with Starting Point Capital are people within my network with whom I have a relationship, and they are learning the benefits of real estate syndications.

The Rise Sun Valley opportunity that I described at the beginning of the book was fully subscribed within six hours after I sent out the invitation and investment summary. That was a personal record. Since then, subsequent opportunities have filled up within a similar time period.

Increasing numbers of investors are turning to passive investing through real estate syndication. They are taking capital from low-interest savings accounts or CDs or making slight changes in their lifestyles to invest in something that creates cash flow and can begin to replace dependence upon active earned income.

If you still cling to traditional mores about investing, know that you do not have to sacrifice diversification if you invest in real estate syndication because opportunities exist not only in multifamily but in self-storage, assisted living, retail, flex office, marinas, or RV parks. And, for the record, I do not advocate putting all your cash into passive real estate investing; there is always room for your favorite stocks, whiskeys, or art. Investing should be fun as well as practical.

Now for the million-dollar question: Is now a good time to invest passively in real estate?

The short answer to this question is *YES!*

For one thing, the United States continues to face a historic housing shortage, and rents are at historic highs. But, if your concern is timing the market fundamentals, consider this.

The rebounds in real estate can be sharp. Just look at 2008, 2009, and 2010. Multifamily took a nosedive, of course, but it was literally 12 months from the time it was declining to bottoming to rebounding. And then the market hit all-time highs. The low point was so short-lived. As the saying goes, the bull takes the stairs, and the bear jumps out the window. It might take eight to ten years to build a full cycle bull market, and then you have a bear market that is sharp, and it is a disaster. But, a year or two later, maybe three at the most, it is rebounding again.

We are seeing this at the time of this writing. Groups like Blackstone are putting $10 billion-plus into the multifamily sector. JP Morgan Chase formed a joint venture and is putting billions into the market. Jeff Bezos is backing a real estate company buying up residential, single-family properties nationwide. It is happening. The big dogs are coming in, and the smart money is buying. So, just take these as signals. These events, coupled with the forecast of rates coming down in the coming years, will only further help to bolster valuations.

Cash-flowing real estate will create a record number of millionaires in the next decade. Are you going to be one of them?

You can learn more about real estate syndication from my podcast, *The Freedom Point Podcast* at:
https://www.startingpointcapital.com/podcast

Please also reach out to me directly to talk about your goals, questions, and future investment opportunities at:
https://www.startingpointcapital.com/about

ABOUT THE AUTHOR

Jeremy Dyer is the managing member of Starting Point Capital (www.startingpointcapital.com). As the managing member, he is also the co-general partner, limited partner, and fund manager in over 4,000 multifamily units with a value of over $500 million. Jeremy is the host of The Freedom Point Podcast for which he has explored the world of passive real estate investing with over 1,200 guests and fellow investors. Jeremy has raised over $30 million for real estate and is a regular contributor to YouTube, LinkedIn, and his blog.

Jeremy leads an exclusive group of affluent passive investors, providing unmatched investment opportunities within a growth-oriented community. He earned a bachelor of science degree in marketing from the Carlson School of Management and went on to consistently attain a top sales professional designation as a high performing sales associate prior to launching his passive real estate investing company.

Lastly, Jeremy is the lifetime husband of Marlene and, together, they live with their four children in Lake Elmo, Minnesota.

APPENDIX

STARTING POINT CAPITAL SPONSOR EVALUATION CRITERIA

When evaluating a general partner (GP) in a real estate investment as a passive limited partner (LP), there are several critical factors to consider. These factors help to ensure the GP has the experience, integrity, and strategy alignment necessary for a successful investment partnership. Here are the most important things to consider when evaluating a general partner.

Experience and Track Record: Evaluate the GP's past performance in similar investments. A strong track record indicates expertise and the ability to navigate various market conditions.

Market Knowledge: The GP should have deep knowledge of the market where the investment is located, understanding local demand, supply, and the regulatory environment.

Investment Strategy: Ensure that the GP's investment strategy aligns with your risk tolerance, investment horizon, and financial goals.

Financial Stability: A GP with strong financial health is better positioned to weather economic downturns and has less need to rely solely upon LP capital.

Transparency: The GP should be open about the investment's financial aspects, risks, and operational status, providing regular, detailed reports.

Communication: Effective and regular communication is key to trust and understanding, ensuring LPs are informed and engaged.

Legal and Regulatory Compliance: The GP must have a clean record of adhering to legal and regulatory requirements, protecting the investment from potential legal issues.

Fees and Compensation Structure: Understand how the GP is compensated to ensure it aligns interests and is fair relative to industry standards.

Due Diligence Process: Evaluate the thoroughness of the GP's due diligence in selecting properties, including financial, physical, and legal inspections.

Asset Management Capabilities: The GP should have a proven ability to manage properties effectively, optimizing operational efficiency and tenant satisfaction.

Risk Management: Assess the GP's strategies for mitigating investment risks, including market, financial, and operational risks.

Exit Strategy: The GP should have a clear, realistic plan for exiting the investment, ensuring alignment with your investment horizon.

Reputation: Consider the GP's reputation in the industry, including feedback from other investors and partners.

Co-Investment: GPs who co-invest with LPs demonstrate confidence in the investment and align interests.

Ethical Standards: The GP should adhere to high ethical standards, ensuring integrity in all aspects of the investment.

Operational Efficiency: Assess the GP's ability to operate properties efficiently, reducing costs and increasing profitability.

Innovation and Adaptability: A GP's ability to innovate and adapt to changing market conditions can protect and enhance investment value.

Networking and Relationships: The GP's relationships with brokers, lenders, and other real estate professionals can provide advantages in sourcing and managing investments.

Team and Expertise: Evaluate the experience and expertise of the GP's team, ensuring they have the skills necessary to manage the investment.

Investor References: Speaking with current or past investors can provide insights into their experience working with the GP.

Conflict of Interest Policies: Ensure the GP has policies in place to manage conflicts of interest fairly.

Technology Utilization: GPs leveraging technology for property management, investor reporting, and market analysis can offer efficiencies and insights.

Portfolio Diversification: Understand how the investment fits within the GP's overall portfolio, assessing diversification and risk concentration.

Alignment of Values: Ensure your personal values and investment philosophy align with the GP's approach and culture.

Support for these evaluation criteria comes from industry best practices and research indicating that these factors are closely correlated with investment success. For example, a strong track record and experience are often cited as key indicators of a GP's ability to deliver returns. Transparency and communication are essential for building trust and ensuring that LPs are informed and engaged in the investment process. Financial stability, ethical standards, and legal compliance protect LPs from potential financial and reputational damage. Lastly, alignment of investment strategy, risk management, and exit plans are critical to meeting LPs' financial goals and investment timelines.

GLOSSARY

1031 EXCHANGE: A swap of one real estate investment property for another that allows capital gains taxes to be deferred.

ABSORPTION RATE: The rate at which available homes are sold in a specific real estate market during a given time period.

ACCREDITED INVESTOR: An individual or entity that meets specific income or net worth requirements as defined by securities regulations. Accredited investors are eligible to participate in certain investment opportunities that may be restricted to non-accredited investors. An accredited investor, according to the terms of the SEC, has a net worth of a million dollars and an income of $200,000 per year if single and $300,000 if married.

AMORTIZATION: The process of spreading out a loan into a series of fixed payments over time. In real estate, it refers to the method by which loan principal decreases over the life of a mortgage.

ARBITRAGE: A strategy to lock in gains by simultaneously purchasing and selling an identical security, commodity, or asset across two different markets.

BRIDGE LOAN: A short-term loan used until a person or company secures permanent financing. It provides immediate cash flow when funding is needed but not yet available.

BROKER OPINION OF VALUE: A broker's opinion of the future value of a property when the renovations are complete. The estimate is often provided to the sponsor or seller during the renovation process.

BUILD TO RENT (BTR): Constructing residential properties with the primary purpose of renting them out to tenants. Unlike traditional real estate development where properties are built for sale, BTR properties are designed to create a consistent stream of rental income.

CAPITAL CALL: A request made by a syndication or fund for a portion of the money promised by an investor, used to fund operations or investment purchases. It is a call for the investor to fulfill their commitment.

CAPITAL EXPENDITURE (CAPEX): Funds used by a company to acquire, upgrade, and maintain physical assets such as property, industrial buildings, or equipment.

CAPITAL IMPROVEMENT: A permanent structural change or restoration that enhances a property's value, extends its useful life, or adapts it to new uses.

CAPITAL STACK: Represents the different types of financing used to purchase and maintain the investment property. It is typically structured from the most senior to the most junior in terms of repayment priority and includes senior debt, mezzanine debt, preferred equity, and common equity.

CAPITALIZATION RATE (CAP RATE): A rate of return on a real estate investment property based upon the expected income that the property will generate. It is used to estimate the investor's potential return on their investment.

CARRIED INTEREST: A share of the syndication's profits that the general partners receive as compensation. It is typically a percentage of the profits earned above a certain return threshold, aligning the interests of the general partner with those of the investors.

CASH FLOW: The income generated from a real estate investment after deducting expenses such as mortgage payments, property management fees, and maintenance costs. Positive cash flow indicates that the property is generating more income than its expenses.

CASH-ON-CASH RETURN: A metric used to calculate the cash income earned on the cash invested in a property. It is determined by dividing the annual pre-tax cash flow by the total cash invested.

CLAWBACK CLAUSE: A provision in a contract that allows for the return of money already paid out, under certain conditions, such as the underperformance of an investment or breach of contract.

CLOSING COSTS: Fees and expenses, over and above the price of the property, that buyers and sellers normally incur to complete a real estate transaction. These costs can include title insurance, attorney fees, appraisals, and transfer taxes.

CO-INVESTMENT: An investment made jointly by multiple investors in a project. In real estate syndications, it can refer to a situation where the sponsor invests their own capital alongside investors.

COMMON AREA MAINTENANCE (CAM): Fees paid by tenants to landlords to cover the costs associated with areas common to all tenants. This can include maintenance and utilities for areas such as lobbies, parking lots, and hallways.

CONCESSION: A discount or incentive offered to a tenant, often used to entice them to sign a lease. Examples include reduced rent for a certain period or a landlord making improvements to the leased space at their own expense.

COST SEGREGATION: A tax strategy used to accelerate depreciation on certain components of a property, allowing investors to reduce their taxable income more quickly. It involves a detailed engineering analysis of the property to identify and reclassify assets into shorter depreciation schedules, rather than the standard depreciation timeline for real estate.

DEBT SERVICE: The total amount of money required to cover the repayment of interest and principal on a debt for a specific time period. It is a key figure in determining the cash flow and profitability of an investment.

DEBT SERVICE COVERAGE RATIO (DSCR): A measure of the cash flow available to pay current debt obligations, calculated by dividing the net operating income by the total debt service. A DSCR of less than one indicates a negative cash flow.

DEPRECIATION: An accounting method of allocating the cost of a tangible asset over its useful life. In real estate, it allows investors to deduct the costs from their taxes, reflecting the property's decrease in value over time.

DEPRECIATION RECAPTURE: The gain realized by the sale of depreciable capital property. Gains must be reported as ordinary income for tax purposes. Depreciation recapture is assessed when the sale price of an asset exceeds the tax basis or adjusted cost basis. The difference between these figures is "recaptured" when it is reported as ordinary income.

DISTRIBUTIONS: Periodic payments made to passive investors from the cash flow generated by the real estate investment. Distributions can be in the form of rental income, profit shares, or other agreed-upon methods.

DISTRIBUTION WATERFALL: The order in which the returns from an investment are distributed to investors. It typically starts with returning the initial capital, followed by a preferred return, and finally the split of remaining profits.

DUE DILIGENCE: The process of conducting thorough research and analysis on a potential real estate investment. This includes evaluating the property's financials, market conditions, tenant history, and legal aspects to assess the risks and potential returns before making an investment decision.

DUE-ON-SALE CLAUSE: A provision in a mortgage or deed of trust that requires the borrower to pay the remaining balance of the loan in full if the property is sold or transferred.

EARNEST MONEY: A deposit made to a seller showing the buyer's good faith in a transaction. It is a part of the purchase price and is held in an escrow account until the deal closes.

EQUITY: The portion of ownership in a property or investment. In real estate, equity represents the value of the property minus any outstanding debts or mortgages.

EQUITY MULTIPLE (EM): A performance metric that measures the total return provided to investors. It is calculated by dividing the total cash distributions received from an investment by the total equity invested.

EQUITY PROFIT SPLIT: Also known as the "promote," the equity profit split describes how the profits from an opportunity are to be distributed among the limited partners and the general partner (sponsor). For example, in an 85-15 split, the limited partners will get 85 percent of the profits and the general partner will receive 15 percent.

ESCROW: An account held by a third party on behalf of the two principal parties in a transaction. In real estate, escrow accounts are commonly used to hold funds for taxes and insurance or to hold the deposit until the transaction is completed.

EXIT CAP RATE: The capitalization rate used to estimate the sell price of a property at the end of the holding period. It helps investors to estimate their potential return when planning to exit the investment.

EXIT STRATEGY: The predetermined plan for selling or exiting the real estate investment. This strategy outlines the time frame and approach to sell the property, potentially realizing capital gains and completing the investment cycle.

FAIR MARKET VALUE: The price that a property would sell for on the open market. It is an estimate of the market value of a property, based upon what a knowledgeable, willing, and unpressured buyer would likely pay to a knowledgeable, willing, and unpressured seller in the market.

FIXED-RATE DEBT: A loan that has a fixed interest rate for the entire term of the loan, providing predictable monthly payments.

FLOATING-RATE DEBT: A loan whereby banks and financial institutions charge a spread over the benchmark rate based on factors such as the type of asset and the consumer's credit rating. A floating rate might be the LIBOR plus 300 basis points.

GENERAL PARTNER (GP): The syndicator or sponsor who takes an active role in managing the real estate investment. General partners often have more significant responsibilities and contribute their expertise and experience to ensure the success of the project.

GOING-IN CAP RATE: The going-in cap rate is the projected first-year Net of Income (NOI) divided by the initial investment or purchase price.

GROSS LEASE: A type of lease where the landlord pays all or most of the property expenses, which may include insurance, taxes, and maintenance, out of the rent received.

GROSS POTENTIAL INCOME (GPI): The total amount of income a rental property would generate if it were fully rented and all rents were collected before any expenses are deducted.

GROSS RENT MULTIPLIER (GRM): A simple measure used to assess the approximate value of an income-producing property. It is calculated by dividing the property's price by its gross rental income.

HARD MONEY LOAN: A loan secured by real property and provided by private investors or companies. These loans typically have higher interest rates than conventional or government loans and are often used for short-term financing.

HOLDING PERIOD: The duration of time an investment is held before it is sold or disposed of. This is significant for determining the capital gains tax rate applicable upon sale.

INTEREST-ONLY LOAN: A loan where the borrower is required to pay only the interest on the principal balance for a set term after which they must repay the principal in full.

INTERNAL RATE OF RETURN (IRR): A financial metric used to estimate the profitability of potential investments. It calculates an annualized rate of growth an investment is expected to generate.

JOINT AND SEVERAL LIABILITY: A legal term that means all parties involved can be held responsible individually or collectively for the full amount of a debt or liability.

JOINT VENTURE (JV): A business arrangement in which two or more parties agree to pool their resources for the purpose of accomplishing a specific task. In real estate, this usually involves investment in a property.

KEY PRINCIPAL: A party with a significant stake in a project, usually required by lenders to have a certain net worth or liquidity to guarantee the loan.

LAZY 1031 EXCHANGE: A provision in the IRS code allowing investors to continue to defer capital gains taxes on the exchange of like-kind properties, usually in the case of large sums of money and high net worth individuals.

LEASEHOLD IMPROVEMENT: Alterations made to rental premises to customize it for the specific needs of a tenant. These improvements will typically revert to the landlord upon termination of the lease.

LEVERAGE: The use of borrowed capital to increase the potential return of an investment. In real estate, this means using mortgage loans to increase the ability to purchase property.

LIEN: A legal right or interest that a lender has in the borrower's property, securing the repayment of a debt or obligation.

LIMITED LIABILITY: A type of investment where a person's financial liability is limited to a fixed sum, most commonly the value of a person's investment in a corporation, company, or partnership.

LIMITED PARTNER (LP): A passive investor in a real estate syndication who contributes capital to the investment but has limited involvement in the decision-making and management of the property. Limited partners typically benefit from potential returns and tax advantages without active participation.

LIQUIDITY: The ability to quickly convert an asset into cash without significantly impacting its price. Real estate is typically considered a less liquid asset.

LOAN COMMITMENT: A lender's promise to offer a loan under specific terms, which includes the loan amount, interest rate, and term.

LOAN-TO-VALUE (LTV) RATIO: A measure used by lenders to assess the risk of a loan. It is calculated by dividing the mortgage amount by the appraised property value.

LOSS TO LEASE: One of the most essential metrics in multifamily real estate, it can be defined as the difference between actual rent and market rent. In general, this income is lost by offering incentives to encourage tenants to sign or renew their lease.

MARKET VALUE: The most probable price that a property should bring in a competitive and open market under all conditions requisite to a fair sale.

MEZZANINE DEBT: A hybrid of debt and equity financing that gives the lender the right to convert to an equity interest in the company in case of default, generally after senior lenders are paid.

NET LEASE: A lease agreement where the tenant agrees to pay a portion or all of the taxes, insurance, and maintenance costs for a property in addition to rent.

NET OPERATING INCOME (NOI): A calculation used to analyze real estate investments that generate income. NOI equals all revenue from the property minus all reasonably necessary operating expenses.

NON-ACCREDITED INVESTOR: An individual or entity that does not meet the income or net worth requirements to be classified as an accredited investor. Non-accredited investors may still have access to certain investment opportunities but may have additional limitations or regulatory requirements.

OFFERING MEMORANDUM (OM): A legal document stating the objectives, risks, and terms of an investment involved with a private placement. This document contains details about the investment property or portfolio.

OPERATING AGREEMENT: An arrangement among a company's members that outlines its business operations and the rights and responsibilities of its members.

OPERATING EXPENSES: Expenses incurred through the operation and maintenance of a property. These can include property management fees, utilities, taxes, and insurance.

PASSIVE REAL ESTATE INVESTING: An investment approach where individuals invest their money in real estate projects but do not actively participate in the management or operations of the property. Instead, they rely upon professional syndicators or sponsors to handle the day-to-day activities.

PORTFOLIO: A range of investments held by a person or organization. In real estate, it refers to a collection of properties owned by an individual, company, or investment group.

POST-CLOSING LIQUIDITY: The amount of liquid assets an investor is required to have after all closing costs and down payments are made. It is often a requirement from lenders to ensure borrowers can cover future financial obligations.

PREFERRED EQUITY: A class of ownership in a corporation that has a higher claim on its assets and earnings than common stock. In real estate, preferred equity investors have priority over common equity investors in terms of distributions.

PREFERRED RETURN: A priority return that must be paid to preferred equity investors before any distributions can be made to other types of equity holders.

PREPAYMENT PENALTY: A fee that lenders might charge if a loan is paid off before the end of its term. It compensates the lender for the interest payments they lose due to early repayment.

PRINCIPAL: The original sum of money borrowed in a loan or the amount of the investment. It can also refer to the main party to a transaction.

PRINCIPAL AND INTEREST: The two components of a mortgage payment. Principal is the portion that pays down the loan balance, and interest is the cost of borrowing the principal.

PRIVATE PLACEMENT MEMORANDUM (PPM): The PPM provides detailed information about the investment opportunity, including the terms, risks, and other pertinent disclosures that potential investors need to consider before making an investment decision. It serves as a comprehensive offering document that outlines the investment opportunity and helps potential investors to make informed choices.

PRO FORMA: A set of financial projections for a real estate investment, which estimates the expected returns, operating expenses, and cash flow.

PROMISSORY NOTE: A financial instrument that contains a written promise by one party to pay another party a definite sum of money either on demand or at a specified future date.

PROMOTE: Also known as the equity profit split, the promote is how the profits from an opportunity are to be distributed among the limited partners and the general partner (sponsor). For example, in an 85-15 split, the limited partners will get 85 percent of the profits, and the general partner will receive 15 percent.

PROPERTY CLASS: Categories used to describe the quality and location of a property. Common classes are A (luxury), B (mid-grade), and C (affordable or older).

PURCHASE AND SALE AGREEMENT (PSA): This is a legal document that outlines the terms and conditions under which the buyer and seller agree to transact the sale of a property. The PSA typically covers the purchase price, closing date, contingencies, financing terms, due diligence period, and any other key terms of the deal.

RATE OF RETURN: The gain or loss on an investment over a specified period expressed as a percentage of the investment's cost.

REAL ESTATE INVESTMENT TRUST (REIT): A company that owns, operates, or finances income-producing real estate. REITs offer a way for investors to receive a share of the income produced through commercial real estate ownership without actually having to buy, manage, or finance any properties themselves.

REAL ESTATE SYNDICATION: A syndication is a group of investors who come together to deploy capital into a project or property. In return for their capital injection, the investor group receives a portion of the cash flow the property produces and the equity upside at the end.

RECOURSE LOAN: A loan where the borrower is personally liable if the funds are not repaid, and the collateral does not cover the full value of the loan.

REFINANCING: The process of replacing an existing loan with a new loan, typically with better terms. In real estate, this is often done to secure a lower interest rate, reduce monthly payments, or tap into a property's equity.

REGULATION D (REG D): A provision under the U.S. federal securities law that allows companies to raise capital through the sale of equity or debt securities without having to register the offering with the SEC, provided they sell only to accredited investors and meet other requirements.

REHABILITATION: The process of improving a property by making repairs or renovations. This can significantly increase the property's value and appeal to tenants or buyers.

RENT ROLL: A document or spreadsheet listing all of the tenants leasing a property, their rent amounts, lease start and end dates, and other key information.

RETURN OF CAPITAL: A distribution to investors from the sponsor that is not based upon profit but a markup added at the initial investment stage. It is designed to manage investor expectations.

RETURN ON CAPITAL: A distribution to investors that is based on real income at the property level.

RETURN ON INVESTMENT (ROI): A measure used to evaluate the efficiency or profitability of an investment, calculated by dividing the net profit of the investment by the initial cost.

RISK ASSESSMENT: The process of identifying and analyzing potential issues that could negatively impact key business initiatives or projects.

RISK TOLERANCE: An individual's capacity to endure loss in their investment values. It is an important factor in determining suitable investment strategies or products.

SCHEDULE K-1: Schedule K-1 is an Internal Revenue Service (IRS) tax form issued annually. It reports the gains, losses, interest, dividends, earnings, and other distributions from certain investments or business entities for the previous tax year. The K-1 form reports each participant's share of the business entity's gains, losses, deductions, credits, and other distributions (whether or not they are actually distributed).

SECURED LOAN: A loan that is backed by collateral, reducing the risk for the lender. In real estate, the property itself typically serves as collateral.

SEED CAPITAL: Capital raised to begin developing an idea for a business or a new product.

SPECIAL PURPOSE VEHICLE (SPV): A special purpose vehicle (SPV) in a fund of funds structure for a single asset is a legal entity created to pool capital from multiple investors and limit their liability to the extent of their investment in the SPV. The SPV's sole purpose is to invest in one particular asset, often directly into the lead sponsor's deal.

SPONSOR: The general partners or operators responsible for sourcing, evaluating, and managing the real estate investment on behalf of the passive investors. The syndicator/sponsor takes the lead in identifying opportunities, negotiating deals, and overseeing the operations of the investment.

STABILIZED PROPERTY: A real estate property that has reached a level of occupancy and income that is sustainable and expected to be maintained over time.

SUBORDINATION CLAUSE: A legal agreement that states that one party's claim or interest is ranked below that of others. In real estate, this often refers to the order of mortgage liens in terms of their priority in being paid off in case of a sale or foreclosure.

SWEAT EQUITY: A term used to describe the value added to a property by the owner through labor and improvements. It is a form of investment that involves effort rather than capital.

SYNDICATE: A group of investors who pool their resources to invest in large projects. In real estate, a syndicate might purchase, develop, or manage property with each member taking a share of the profits and losses.

SYNDICATION: A temporary professional financial services alliance formed for the purpose of handling a large transaction that would be hard or impossible for the entities involved to handle individually. In real estate, it refers to pooling capital from multiple investors to purchase a property.

SYNDICATION OFFERING: The comprehensive document that provides detailed information about a specific real estate investment opportunity. The offering includes property details, financial projections, terms of the investment, and other relevant information for potential passive investors to review before making an investment decision.

SYNDICATOR: The individual or entity responsible for sourcing, evaluating, and managing the real estate investment on behalf of the passive investors. The syndicator/sponsor takes the lead in identifying opportunities, negotiating deals, and overseeing the operations of the investment.

TENANT IMPROVEMENT ALLOWANCE (TIA): An agreed upon amount of money that the landlord is willing to spend towards the improvement of an interior space to meet the tenant's requirements.

TERM LOAN: A loan from a bank for a specific amount that has a specified repayment schedule and a fixed or floating interest rate.

TITLE: The legal right to own, use, and dispose of property. Title also refers to the documents that record the ownership of the property and the history of property transactions.

TITLE INSURANCE: An insurance policy that protects real estate owners and lenders against any property loss or damage they might experience because of liens, encumbrances, or defects in the title to the property.

TRAILING 12 MONTHS (TTM): A term that describes the past 12 consecutive months of a company's performance. The data gives a more current picture of a business's financial performance than its annual filings and reports, which, at times, can contain information that is more than a year old.

UNDERCAPITALIZED: A situation in which a business has insufficient capital to support its operations and growth. In real estate, it might refer to a property owner not having enough funds to maintain or improve the property.

UNDERWRITING: The process of evaluating and assessing the risk to an investor of making a loan, issuing an insurance policy, or making a securities investment.

VACANCY RATE: The percentage of all available units in a rental property, such as an apartment complex or office building, that are vacant or unoccupied at a particular time.

VALUE-ADD: A strategy in real estate where investors seek out properties that have the potential for increased income through renovations, rebranding, or improvements in management.

VARIABLE INTEREST RATE: An interest rate on a loan or security that fluctuates over time because it is based on an underlying benchmark interest rate or index that changes periodically.

VESTING: The process by which an employee accrues non-forfeitable rights over employer-provided stock incentives or employer contributions made to the employee's retirement plan account.

WATERFALL STRUCTURE: A method of distributing the cash flow from an investment that prioritizes different tiers of investors. Each tier must be fully paid in the sequence of distribution before moving on to the next tier.

YIELD: The income return on an investment such as the interest or dividends received from holding a particular security. In real estate, it is often referred to as the yield on cost or the current yield.

YIELD MAINTENANCE: Yield maintenance dictates that borrowers pay the rate differential between the loan interest rate and the prevailing market interest rate on the prepaid capital for the period remaining to loan maturity.

YIELD SPREAD: The difference between yields on different debt instruments, adjusted for the fact that they may have different credit ratings or maturities. In real estate, it might refer to the difference in yield between a property investment and a risk-free rate of return.

ZONING: Regulations established by local governments regarding the use of land and the types of buildings allowed in different areas. Zoning laws can significantly affect real estate development and property values.

Made in the USA
Columbia, SC
09 June 2025